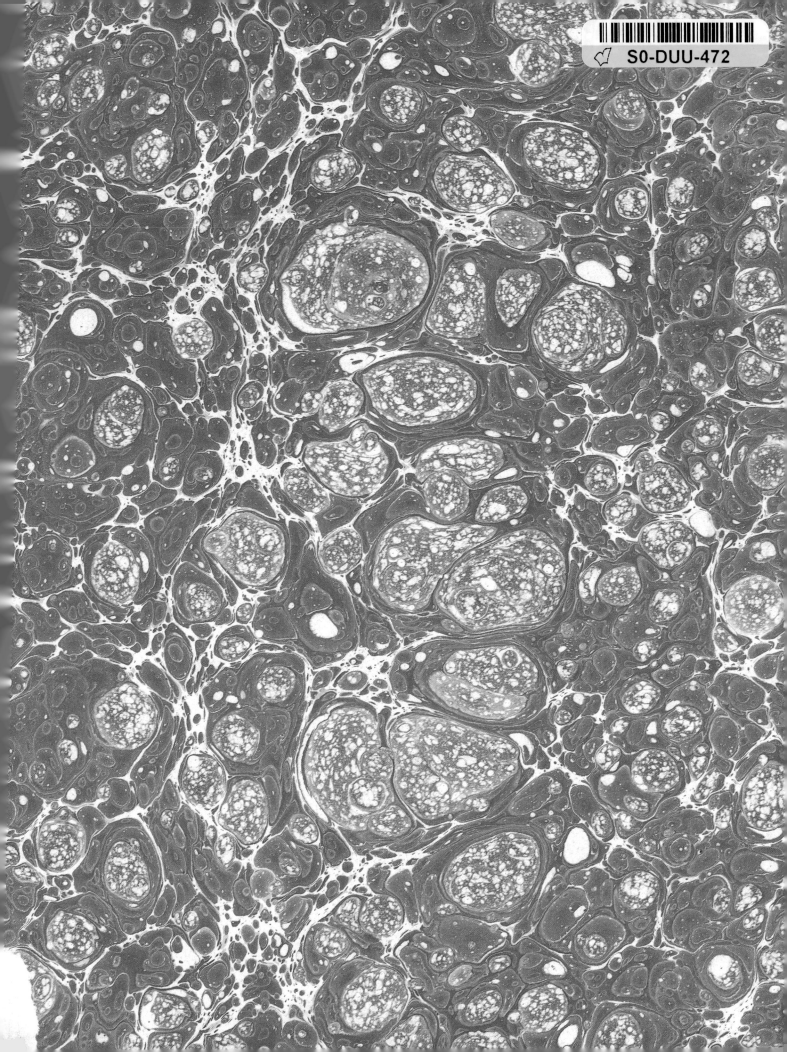
S0-DUU-472

ENCYCLOPEDIA

OF

ANTIQUE ADVERTISING

VOLUME II

By RAY KLUG

Schiffer Publishing Ltd

1469 Morstein Road, West Chester, Pennsylvania 19380

E
161
.K58
1985
v.2

LIBRARY

NATURAL HISTORY MUSEUM
OF LOS ANGELES COUNTY

Copyright © 1985 by Ray Klug.
Library of Congress Catalog Number: 00-00000.

All rights reserved. No part of this work may be
reproduced or used in any forms or by any means—
graphic, electronic or mechanical, including
photocopying or information storage and retrieval
systems—without written permission from the
copyright holder.

Printed in the United States of America.
ISBN: 0-88740-141-4
Published by Schiffer Publishing Ltd.
1469 Morstein Road, West Chester, Pennsylvania 19380
Formerly published by L-W Book Sales
Box 69, Gas City, Indiana 46933

This book may be purchased from the publisher.
Please include $2.00 postage.
Try your bookstore first.

TABLE OF CONTENTS

PREFACE

Well, here we go a few years and a few more miles up the road and another Antique Advertising book. I really had no intention of doing another book after the last one, but my publisher is a very persistent person and after many phone calls, he finally got my okay. I was a little slow getting started but then there came more phone calls upon more phone calls with hurry, hurry and I picked up the pace a bit. I'm about a year behind but here it is, and I like what came out. I've been asked so many times throughout the years about using color. It is very expensive but we went ahead and used a great deal of color in the book.

I'd like to call your attention to the cover photo. You know that selecting a cover photo isn't easy, as there are many great items to choose from. I knew when I first saw this sign that this was it. I think it is one of the finest examples of Early American Advertising I've ever seen. Herb and Elaine Ashendorf are the owners of this sign and had it professionally photographed for the cover of this book.

Early Advertising today is as much sought after as ever. There are Antique Advertising shows each year from coast to coast. These are specialty shows and are well attended by the public, dealers, decorators, and collectors. Advertising in some form can also be found at just about any of the Flea Markets and Antique Shows in the country today.

As I have said in Volume I, I still find many dealers asking astronomical prices for advertising items in very poor condition. Condition is the main factor in pricing and I cannot emphasize enough, DO NOT OVER-RATE CONDITION. I know when we own it, we have a tendency to think it is better condition than it is. Don't fool yourself.

For the new collectors who do not own Volume I, I'd like to say there are three Advertising Clubs open for membership. These are: Tin Containers Collectors Association (T.C.C.A.), The National Association Breweriana Advertising (N.A.B.A), and The Cola Clan (T.C.C.). The monthly newsletters of these clubs are very informative and easily justify the small cost of membership. I highly recommend the joining of these clubs. Conventions are also held by all clubs.

Next, do not attempt to repair early advertising if your are an amateur. I have seen a great amount of good advertising just about ruined by amateurs. Never us tape, household glue or lacquer. Leave the item as it is. You are not only hurting the items, but yourself, by lowering the value with repair that cannot be corrected. All repair work should be left for the experts only.

I've heard many times over the past few years how hard it is to find Antique Advertising. True, there isn't as much choice advertising as there was in the beginning as so much has been used by decorators and bought up for collections. The Antique Advertising Shows are your best bet for finding what you need. Those who have attended a show for the first time are awed at the great amount of merchandise to be found. There are many, many good buys at these shows. I might add, if you've never attended one of these shows, you really should find the time, as they are well worth the trip and time.

Antique Advertising covers a very broad field and many times an Antique dealer will have advertising and be unaware of it. Just about anything found in an old store or building (no matter what the business was) falls in the advertising category. To name a few: store lights, lamps, shades, windows, doors, architectural items, mirrors, some furniture, boxes, baskets, etc. Other items that can be found at the shows are advertising dolls, toys, banks, dishes, glassware, celluloid buttons, coolers, clocks, etc. There never seems to be an end to all the things that can be found. Each and every show brings items that have never been seen before. I think the Advertising shows are the most unique of all the antique shows.

As I look back over the past sixteen years of dealing in advertising, I find I have many memories, good and bad. There were also days of sitting on the highway trapped in deep snow and the time I went across the desert in the afternoon without an air conditioner. That one really did me in! Then there were shows in large barren lots with the temperature at one hundred, shows in the winter in unheated buildings, and in the summer without air conditioning The bad things that happened then, don't seem that bad today. My fondest memories are those of the thousands of friends I've met throughout the years. There are those who have shared their home with me as we discussed advertising until the early morning hours, and of course those who have shared my home.

After my first book was published, I was in Indianapolis and the publisher asked me to go to dinner. We took my truck and when he got in, he had to move my camera which was laying on the seat. He picked it up and said, "What's this?" I replied, "My camera". He said, "You don't mean to tell me you took all those pictures with this thing?". I said "YUP". It was a $25 polaroid. He promptly got a good one for me which I still use today. All of these things are associated with my books directly or indirectly. There will probably be more books in the future. In the meantime, I hope you enjoy the book I've put together for you.

Ray Klug

ACKNOWLEDGEMENTS

I wish to express my deepest thanks to the following friends, dealers, and collectors whose help has made this book possible:

Rick and Josie Lee-Lincoln, Mass.
Phil and Karol Atkinson-Mercer Penn.
George and Dolly Yanolko-Allentown, Penn.
Bob and Beka Mebane-San Antonio, Texas
Dave Harris (Hoosier Peddler)-Kokomo, IN
Gloria Evers-Marion, Ohio
Vic, Tom and Bob Hug-Lorain, Ohio
Cubberley's Inc.-Marion, IN
Bo and Susan Franks-Austin, Texas
Allan Katz-Woodbridge, Conn.
Herb and Elaine Ashendorf-Yonkers, New York
Mike Goyda-East Petersburg, Penn.
Don and Pam Lurito-Cambridge, Mass.
John Lucas-Marion, Ohio
Bill and Amy Vehling-Indianapolis, IN
Neil S. Wood-Gas City, IN
Jane Conder-Anderson, IN

A GUIDE TO GRADING

For those who prefer using the scale system of one to ten.

(1) VERY VERY POOR - Ninety per cent wiped out with rust, scratches, dents, fading. Has no value. Less than good condition.

(2) GOOD CONDITION - Small scratches or pitting, small dents, small rust spots. Not usually collected unless an early or rare tray, sign or tin.

(3) GOOD CONDITION PLUS - Better than Good Condition but less than Very Good Condition.

(4) VERY GOOD CONDITION - Minor scratches or flaking, ring stains or stains, minor fading of color. Very minor dents, rust, if any, must be minor, pin head size, not on main part of picture.

(5) VERY GOOD CONDITION PLUS - Better than Very Good Condition but less than Fine Condition.

(6) FINE CONDITION - A fine tray, sign or tin will have minor hairlines scratches on surface, medium paint chipping on edge, very minor fading, possibley and faint ring stain or stain. NO RUST!!

(7) FINE CONDITION PLUS - Better than Fine Condition but less than Excellent, Near New Condition.

(8) EXCELLENT, NEAR NEW CONDITION - Appears to be new, but on close examination will have hairlines on the surface of the tray, sign or tin. Minor paint chipping on the rim or edges. Many dealers call this mint. It is not Mint. It is New.

(9) EXCELLENT, NEAR NEW CONDITION PLUS - Better than Excellent, Near New Condition but less than Mint or New Condition.

(10) MINT OR NEW CONDITION - No trace of handling. Absolutely new. To be in this condition, tray, sign or tin would have to be found in original wrapper.

SCALE CHART

10 - Mint or New Condition
9 - Excellent, Near New Condition Plus
8 - Excellent, Near New Condition
7 - Fine Condition Plus
6 - Fine Condition
5 - Very Good Condition Plus
4 - Very Good Condition
3 - Good Condition Plus
2 - Good Condition
1 - Very Very Poor

NOTE

Special attention should be given to this grading guide. Many dealers and collectors have a tendency to over-rate condition of an item. Particular attention should be given to the fading of an item. Throughout the years, many signs, tins and trays have faded. In most cases, sunlight or just plain light have caused the items to fade. Fading in some cases have caused items to turn a completely different color. This is confusing for the person who has never seen the item in new condition. For those who do not wish to use the scale, use numbers 2,4,6,8 & 10.

SIZES

SIZES - Sizes have been rounded out to the closest quarter inch.

SIZES FOR SIGNS - Length then Height

SIZES FOR TINS, BINS, MISC. - Length, Depth, & Height

SIZES FOR HEINZ FOOD PRODUCT CONTAINERS ARE FOR HEIGHT

SIZES FOR POT AND PAN SCRAPERS - are given only for the smallest 2½" x 3¼" and the largest 3¼" x 2½" inches.

There are some items in this book that are not sized. Sizes were not available at the time of printing. A value has been placed on these items.

If a number is skipped such as 113 goes to 115, number 114 photo could not be processed.

PRICING - All items are numbered and priced in separate price guide, the same as Volume I.

DATES - Most of the items in this book are not dated. I could guess to within a few years on most, but this I will not do. I've place dates only on the dated items. Most are between 1885 and 1945. All are old.

PHOTOGRAPHY - Seventy-five per cent of the items in this book were photographed by the author.

COLOR - A great deal of color photographs have been added to this Volume II so you can enjoy the item in its entirety.

MUSIC - This is a new addition and features some original art work along with many of the Big Band leaders such as Glenn Miller, Tommy Dorsey, Vaughn Monroe, Tommy Tucker, Jimmy Dorsey, etc.

BREWERY - This is a continuation to brewery items found in Volume I. A lot of color and many choice items can be found in this section.

HEINZ FOOD CONTAINERS - Heinz food items being highly collectible, have been added to this Volume II. You'll find these containers are not cheap to collect.

POT AND PAN SCRAPERS - This too, is a new addition. Once used to scrape your pots and pans, many have survived amd surfaced to find their way into many collections. Many companies took advantage of these little metal scrapers and advertised on them. Some had the same front side but were different on the back side. These are much sought after.

PEANUT BUTTER PAILS - These are a continuation from Volume I. There are many prized pails pictured in this section.

CHRISTMAS PAILS - These too, are a new addition. The selection is small but puts one aware of the value of these pails. Most were given away at your local grocer and contained candy.

CIGAR CUTTERS AND LIGHTERS - Here again, we have a new addition. I've been asked many times over about cigar cutters and lighters. This selection is tops in every way.

MATCH HOLDERS - These too are a continuation from Volume I. You'll find some very choice match holders pictured here.

MOXIE ITEMS - Another new addition. Many soft drink companies in the early years advertised their products as being a medicinal help. Moxie was called a nerve food, Coca-Cola was the ideal brain tonic and Pepsi-Cola was healthful and invigorating. Things soon changed and these companies, along with many others, began selling their products as soft drinks. Moxie items are very much sought after and I've pictured some great pieces for you.

DOOR PUSHES - Here is another continuation from Volume I. Once tacked to the doors of general stores, drug stores and saloons, this little plate has found its way into the homes of many collectors. Being small in size it takes very little room to collect them.

GUM MACHINES - A rare selection of L shaped gum machines has been photographed and is also a new addition. These machines are hard to find and are much sought after.

CLOCKS - Not too many, but you'll find a rare Sidney Advertising Clock and a rare Chief Bonus Tea (Baird Clock) along with some other fine examples.

TRAYS - There are choice brewery trays among others to be found in this selection. A continuation from Volume I.

SIGNS - Medicinal, gunpowder, whiskey, tobacco, product, music, brewery, etc. Some of the finest examples in the country are in this book. You'll find two Gold Dust, a Hoffman House Whiskey, Davis Pain Killer, Campbell's Soup and a super Bull Durham just to name a few.

TINS - The tin containers are very limited as many were pictured in Volume I.

MISCELLANEOUS - This section is packed with many hard to get items. A Western Union Lamp, Display cases and items, Machines, Modox Glasses, Papier-mache, Jars, and much, much more.

ADVERTISING CLUBS
For those wishing to join, write:

NATIONAL ASSOCIATION OF BREWERIANA ADVERTISING
C/O Robert Jaeger
2343 Met-To-Wee Lane
Wauwatosa, WI 53226

TIN CONTAINER COLLECTORS ASSOCIATION
Peter Sidlow
11650 Riverside Drive
North Hollywood, CA 91602

THE COLA CLAN
Mrs. Alice Fisher
2084 Continental Dr. N.E.
Atlanta, GA 30345

About the Author

   Mr. Klug was born and raised in Akron, Ohio. He was a bar and restaurant owner in the sixties. During this period of time he began buying antiques and bottles. Throughout the years, he found that his love for antiques superseded that of being a bar and restaurant owner. In 1965 he sold his business and opened a bottle shop. Along with the bottles came signs and tin containers which he quickly showed a preference for. His first advertising buy was a gunpowder calendar, his next a case of old toothpowder tins. Thus started his career in early advertising. A few years later on March 25, 26th, 1972, the first all Antique Advertising Show was held at Indianapolis. Mr. Klug and L-W Promotions were the promoters of the show, which remains yet today. It is the number one advertising show in the country. Throughout the years, Mr. Klug has put together four Antique Advertising books, this being his fifth. He has become one of the country's foremost authorities on Antique Advertising. He is a big band buff and a collector of the big band memorabilia.

Neil S. Wood

Check your trade publications
for other shows promoted by
L-W PROMOTIONS

Box 69, Gas City, IN. 46933

BS-135 A.B.C. Beer
Tin & Wood 29" x 28"

BS-136 Akron Brewing Co.
Wood 26" x 24"

BS-137 Alamo (Lone Star Brewery)
Tin 16½" x 22"

BS-141 Alamo Girl (Lone Star)
Tin 19" x 25½"

BS-142 American Brewing Co.
Reverse on Glass

BS-143 Anchor Brewing Co.
Copper 21" x 17"

BS-146 Banner Brewery
Paper 28" x 22"

BS-148 Bartholomay's Brewery
Paper 20" x 26"

BS-150 Bergner & Eugel Brewery Tin

BS-151 Bernheimer & Schwartz Brewing Co.
Paper 30" x 22"

BS-153 Boston Beer Co.
Porcelain 24"

BS-154 Christian Brecht Brewery
Paper 14" x 23"

BS-157 Buckeye Brewing Co.
Brass 20" x 14"

BS-162 M. Burkhardt Brewing
Tin Self Framed 33" x 23"

BS-161 Budweiser
Tin Self Framed 26" x 38"

BS-163 Carney Lynch & Co.
Paper 31" x 24"

BS-164 Centlivre's Beer
Paper 19" x 24"

BS-165 Cold Spring Brewing Co.
Paper 14" x 20"

BS-166 Consumers Brewing Co.
Paper 31" x 20"

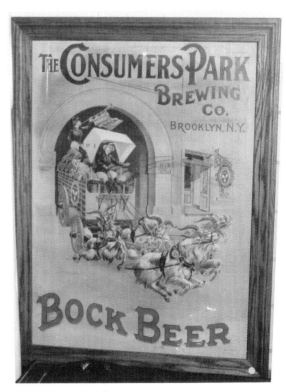

BS-167 Consumers Park Brewing Co. Paper

BS-169 Jos. Doelger's Sons
Tin 20" x 27"

BS-170 Peter Doelger Brewery
Paper 14" x 20"

BS-172 Eagle Brewing Co.
Curtiss Flight Paper
Calendar 1911 23½" x 29½"

BS-173 Ferd Effinger's Brewery Tin

BS-172A Edelweiss Beer
Paper 21" x 31"

17

BS-174 Eigenbrot Brewery
Tin Corner Sign 13" x 20"

BS-178 Germania Brewing Co.
Porcelain Corner Sign 15" x 22"

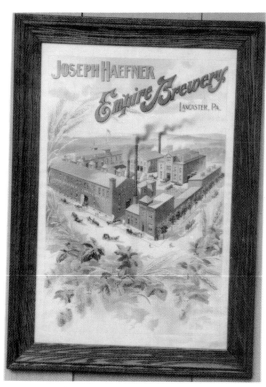

BS-182 Joseph Haefner Brewery
Paper 27" x 18"

BS-184 Chr. Heurich Brewing
Reverse on Glass 25" x 20"

BS-185 Hinckel Lager Beer
Tin 27" x 19½"

BS-186 Hoster Brewing Co.
Paper 16" x 24"

BS-188 L. Hoster Brewing Co.
Paper 40" x 27"

BS-189 Hudepohl Brewing Co.
Milk Glass Corner Sign 23" x 16"

BS-191 Indianapolis Brewing Co.
Paper 27" x 21"

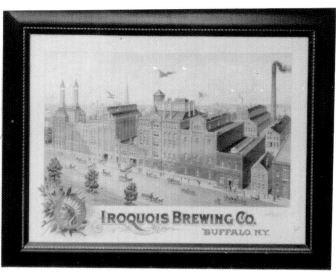

BS-192 Iroquois Brewing Co.
Paper 42" x 32"

BS-193 Jetter Brewing Co.
Tin Self Framed

BS-195 Frank Jones Brewery
Paper 32" x 20"

BS-196 Frank Jones Brewing Co.
Paper 14" x 20"

BS-197 Frank Jones Brewing Co.
Paper 15" x 20"

BS-198 Jung Brewing Co.

BS-199 Kamm & Schellinger Brewing Co.
Paper 24" x 30"

BS-200 J.W. Kenney Park Brewery
Paper 15" x 20"

BS-201 Kessler Brewing Co.
Paper 21½" x 26"

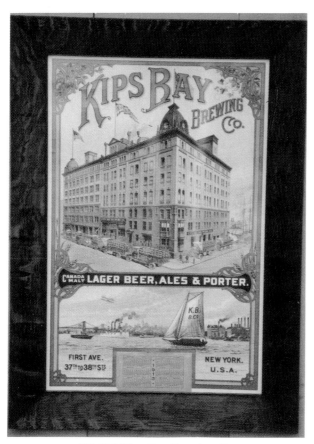

BS-202 Kips Bay Brewing Co.
Paper 26" x 17"

BS-203 John H. Kurth & Co.
Embossed Tin 13¾" x 27½"

BS-205 Lauer Brewing Co.
Paper 42" x 27"

BS-206 Issaac Leisy & Co.
Paper 32" x 36"

BS-208 Lembeck & Betz
Paper 20" x 26"

BS-207 Leisy's Brewing Co.
Tin Self Framed 30½" x 22½"

BS-212 Loyalhanna Brewing Co.
Tin 46½" x 34"

BS-213 Loyalhanna Brewing Co.
Tin-Wood Frame 46" x 34"

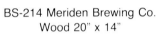

BS-214 Meriden Brewing Co.
Wood 20" x 14"

BS-215 Middletown Brewery
Paper 29" x 22"

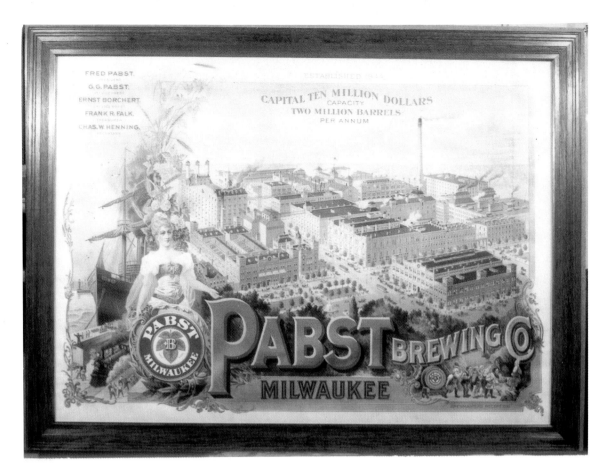

BS-220A Pabst Brewing Co. Paper 43" x 21"

BS-213A McCormick Brewing Co. Tin 24"

BS-216 Minnesota City Brewery Paper 24" x 30"

BS-219 Mooser Brewing Co.
Porcelain Corner Sign 27" x 13"

BS-220 Narragansett Brewery Tin
Self Framed 22" x 17"

BS-224 H. & J. Pfaff
Paper 27" x 23"

BS-226 Rainier Beer Paper

BS-229 Renner & Weber Brewing Porcelain
Corner Sign 25" x 18"

BS-231 Rochester Brewing Co.
Paper 32" x 36"

BS-232 Roessle Brewery Paper 28" x 20"

BS-233 San Antonio Brewery
Paper 19" x 25"

BS-234 Schlather Beer Cleveland & Sandusky
Brewery Reverse on Glass Corner Sign 16" x 21"

BS-235 Schlitz Famo
Tin 8¾" x 19"

BS-236 Schmulbach Beer
Reverse on Glass 16" x 22"

BS-241 Union Brewing & Malting Co. Tin Self Framed
20½" x 17"

BS-244 Weisbrod & Hess Paper 1908 29" x 20"

BS-246 D. G. Yuengling Brewing
Paper 20" x 15"

TOBACCO SIGNS

TS-161 Admiral Cigarettes Paper 31½" x 23½"

TS-162 Allen & Ginter Tobacco
Paper 21½" x 28½"

TS-163 Allen & Ginter Tobacco
Paper 20¾" x 29¼"

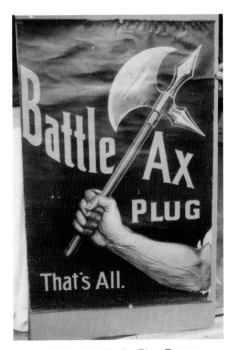

TS-164 Battle Ax Plug Paper

TS-168 Black & Tan Tobacco
Paper 13" x 21"

TS-170 Bloomer Club Cigar Paper

TS-175 Challenge Tobacco Cardboard 15½" x 20½"

TS-180 Five Brothers Plug Tin 16" x 16"

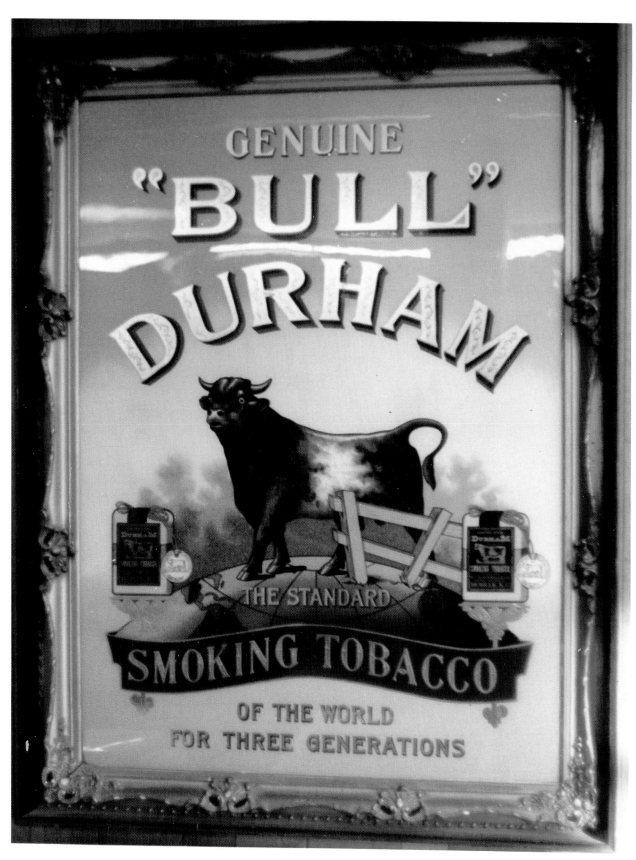

TS-173A Bull Durham Reverse on Glass Molded Frame 44" x 56"
Owned by Cubberley's Inc. Marion, Indiana

TS-176 Continental Tobacco Tin 12" x 16"

TS-181 Haworth & Williams Cigars
Paper 11½" x 14½"

TS-183 Helmar Cigarettes Paper

TS-184 Hoffman House Cigar Paper 21½" x 27"

TS-185 Honest Tobacco
Paper 21" x 29"

TS-189 P. Lorillard & Co. Paper 12" x 14"

TS-187 C.A. Jackson & Co. Tobacco Tin 26" x 38"

TS-186 Iroquois Cigar Paper

TS-190 P. & G. Lorillard Paper 15" x 20"

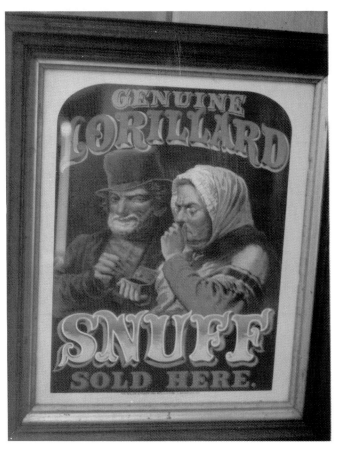

TS-191 Lorillard Snuff Paper 12" x 14"

TS-194 D.H. McAlpin & Co. Paper 18" x 23"

TS-195 Mechanic's Delight
Heavy Paper 17¾" x 26"

TS-196 L. Miller & Sons
Tin 10" x 13½"

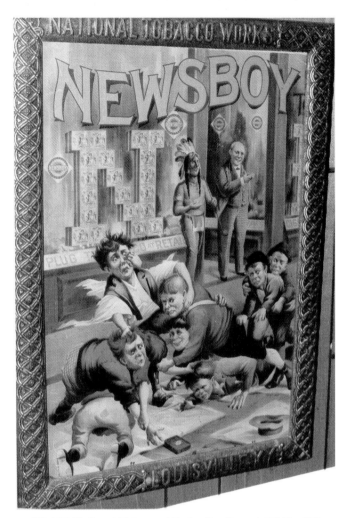

TS-199 National Tobacco Works Cardboard 19½" x 27"

TS-203 Octagon Cigars Tin 18" x 24"

TS-204 Old English Curve Cut Paper-Wood Frame 43" x 64"

TS-205 Old Virginia Cheroots Paper 17" x 16"

TS-207 S. Ottenberg & Bros. Cigars Tin 10" x 13½"

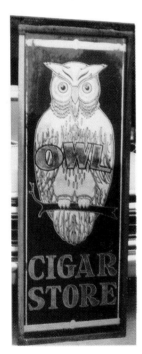

TS-208 Owl Cigar Store
Reverse on Glass
30¼" x 80"

TS-209 Perfection Cigarettes Paper

TS-211 Pinch Hit Tobacco
Cardboard

TS-213 Red Man Tobacco Paper 45" x 31½"

TS-214 Richmond Cigarettes Tin

TS-216 Capt. Sigsbee Cigar Tin 17½" x 23½"

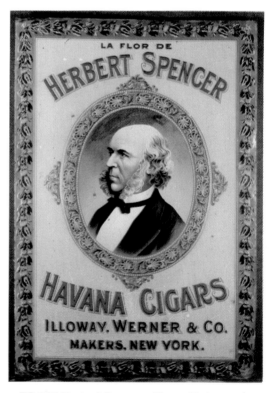

TS-217 Herbert Spencer Cigars Embossed
Tin 14" x 20"

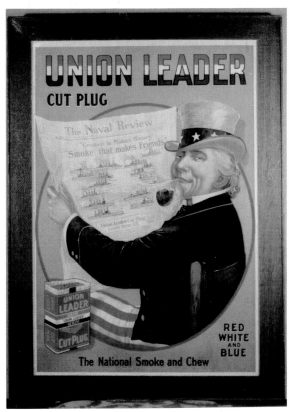

TS-221 Union Leader Cardboard 18" x 26"

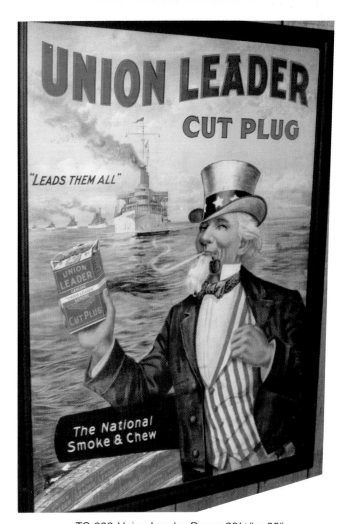

TS-222 Union Leader Paper 28½" x 38"

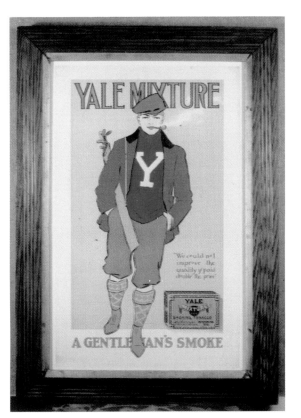

TS-225 Yale Mixture
Paper 14" x 22"

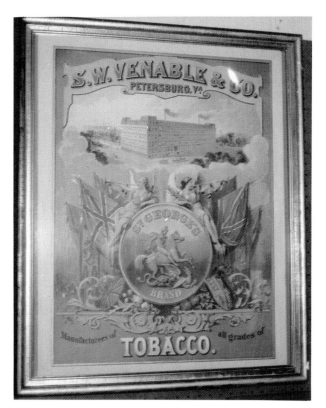

TS-224 S.W. Venable & Co. Paper

MDS-1 Allan's Anti-Fat
Paper 23" x 29"

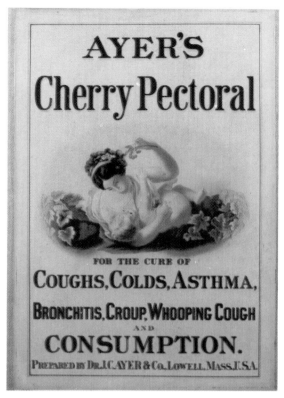

MDS-3 Ayer's Cherry Pectoral
Tin 14" x 20"

MDS-5 Ayer's Pills Paper 30" x 42"

MDS-4 Ayer's Cherry
Pectoral Paper
30" x 42"

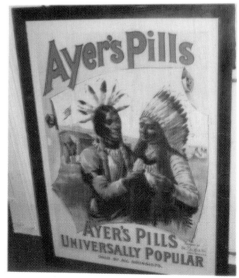

MDS-6 Ayer's Pills Paper 30" x 42"

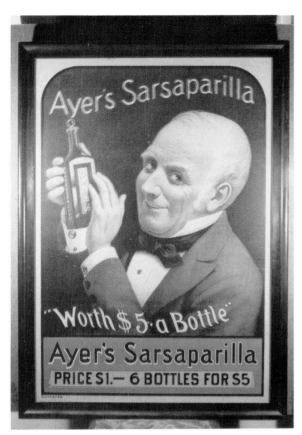

MDS-8 Ayer's Sarsparilla Cardboard 30" x 42"

MDS-9 Ayer's Sarsaparilla
Cardboard 30" x 42"

MDS-11 Boericke & Tafel Paper 22" x 28"

MDS-12 Boschees German Syrup Tin 19" x 27"

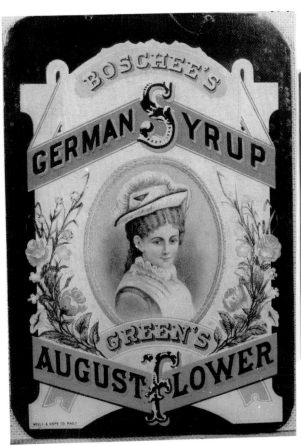

MDS-13 Boschee's German Syrup Tin 7" x 10"

MDS-14 Boschee's German Syrup Greens August Flower
Tin 20" x 14"

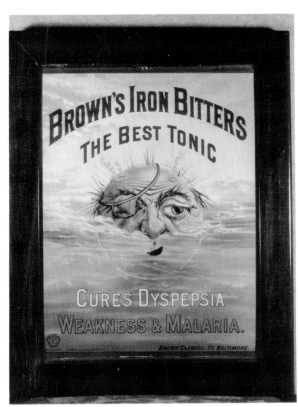

MDS-15 Brown's Iron Bitters Paper 14" x 18"

MDS-22 Dr. A. C. Daniels Paper 16" x 22"

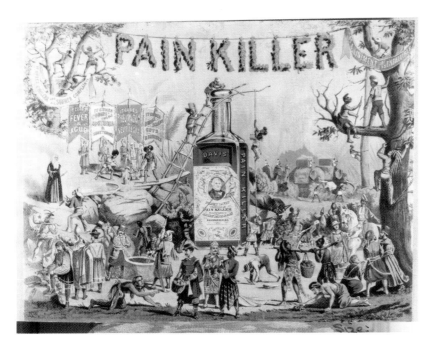

MDS-24 Davis Pain Killer Tin 24" x 18"

MDS-24A Ex-Lax
Porcelain Ther-
mometer 8" x 28"

MDS-28 Green's Ague Conqueror Tin 27½" x 20"

MDS-29 Green's August Flower Tin 31" x 28"

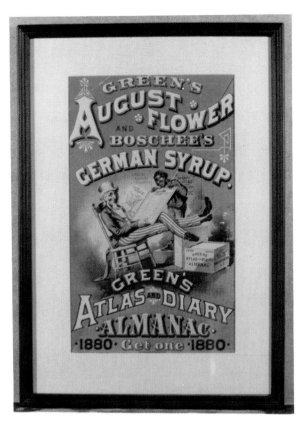

MDS-32 Green's August Flower Paper 9" x 14"

MDS-34 Dr. Hobbs Sparagus
Kidney Pills Paper 14" x 17"

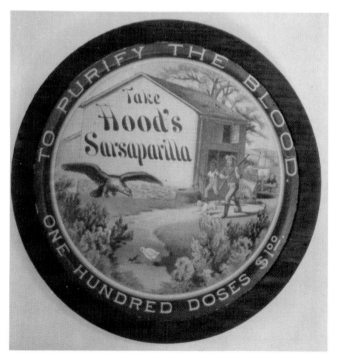

MDS-35 Hoods Sarsaparilla Cardboard 9"

MDS-39 Lash's Bitters Tin Die Cut

MDS-49 Quaker Bitters Paper 18" x 13"

MDS-50 Rex Bitters Cardboard 9" x 12"

MDS-51 Rock, Rye and Honey Cardboard

MDS-53 Tarrant's Aperient Tin 18" x 24"

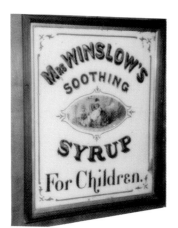

MDS-62 Mrs. Winslow's
Syrup Reverse on Glass
20" x 24"

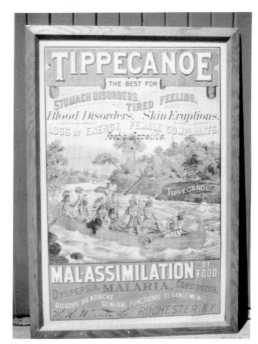

MDS-54 Tippecanoe (Cover Picture)
Paper 42" x 26"

MDS-55 Wa-Hoo Bitters Paper

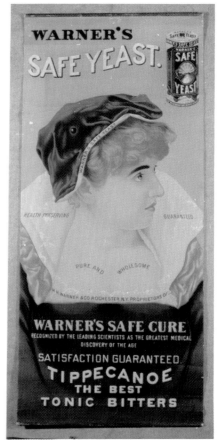

MDS-59 Warner's Safe Yeast
Paper 18" x 28"

WHISKEY SIGNS

WS-83 Belle of Milton Whiskey

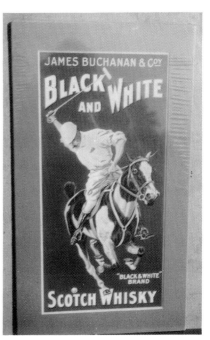

WS-84 Black & White Scotch
Whiskey Paper

WS-86 Buffalo Club Rye Whiskey
Tin 23½" x 33½"

WS-88 Diamond Wine Co. Paper 19" x 27"

WS-89 Eagle Liqueur Distilleries Paper 20" x 25"

WS-92 I.W. Harper Reverse on Glass 40" x 50"

WS-93 I.W. Harper's Whiskey Brass Corner
Sign 12" x 15"

WS-94 Hoffman House Rye Heavy Metal
13" x 19"

WS-96 Mallard Distilling Co. Tin Self Framed
28¼" x 22½"

WS-98 Old Capitol Rye Paper

WS-99 Old Picker Whiskey Paper 21½" x 25½"

WS-101 Jos. E. Pepper Dis. Co. Tin 33" x 45"

WS-104 Rooney's Malt Whiskey Tin 20" x 24"

WS-105 Royal Ruby Rye Reverse on Glass
12" x 18"

WS-107 White Star Pure Rye
Tin 14" x 19"

WS-106 VVE. P. Savard, Georgeon & Co. Tin
Self Framed 13½" x 19"

WS-108 Wright & Taylor Whiskey Tin 24" x 24"

MISCELLANEOUS SIGNS

MS-265 Adams Chewing
Gum Tin 9½" x 13½"

MS-276 Armour's
Veribest Beans Tin
24½" x 14¼"

MS-270 American Beauty Malt Extract
Cardboard

MS-271 American Stock Food Paper

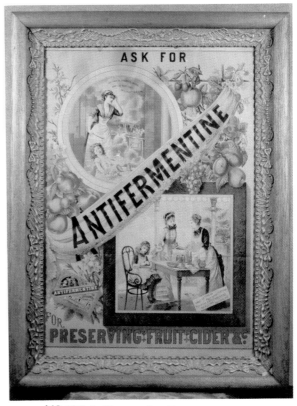

MS-273 Antifermentine Paper 24" x 30"

MS-277 Armour's Mince Meat Tin 21½" x 27¾"

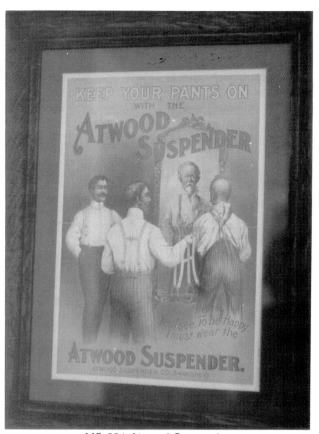

MS-281 Atwood Suspender
Paper 11" x 16"

MS-284 Aunt Jemima's Pancake
Flour Cardboard 8" x 17½"

MS-285 Austin's Dog Bread Tin 26" x 38"

MS-286 B.T. Babbitt's Soap
Paper 14½" x 29"

54

MS-287 B.T. Babbitt's Soap
Cardboard 13½" x 19"

MS-289 Walter Baker & Co. Paper 27" x 23"

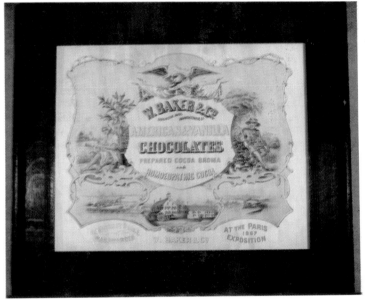

MS-290 W. Baker & Co. Paper 24" x 19"

MS-291 W.H. Baker Paper 14" x 24"

MS-292 Walter Baker & Co.
Embossed Tin 9½" x 6½"

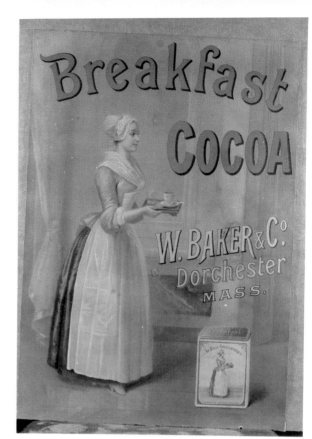

MS-295 W. Baker & Co. Paper 17" x 24"

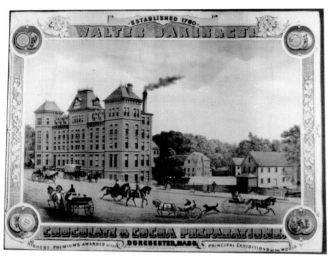

MS-294 Walter Baker & Co. Paper 30" x 23"

MS-296 Walter Baker & Co. Tin 14" x 20"

MS-297 W. Baker & Co.
Plaster 17" x 21"

MS-306 D. Bernhard's
Cardboard 13" x 20"

MS-307 Best Baking Co. Cardboard 12" x 14½"

MS-309 Geo. H. Bishop & Co. Tin

MS-312 Bon-Ton Corset Cardboard Date 1881
13½" x 18"

MS-310 Black Cat Shoe Dressing-Polish Tin
Actual Clock

MS-318 Brown's Shoes Embossed Tin
19½" x 14"

MS-313 Boston Daily & Sunday Globe Embossed
Tin 11" x 17"

MS-325 E. Burnham's Toilet
Requisites Paper 12" x 16"

MS-327 Burt & Packard Shoes
Embossed Tin

MS-330 Cadbury's Cocoa Porcelain 48" x 36"

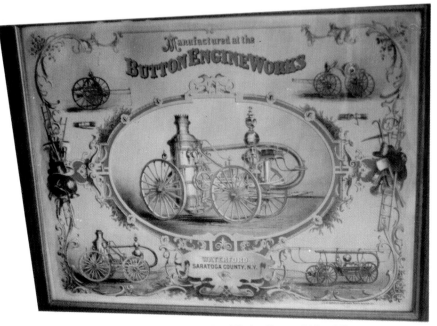

MS-328 Button Engine Works Paper 23" x 18"

MS-331 California Amusement Park Paper 24" x 36"

MS-339 J. & P. Coats Paper 24" x 20"

MS-333 Campbell's Soups Embossed Tin 48" x 36"

MS-336 Clark's O.N.T. Canvas 20½" x 13½"

MS-337 Cloverine
Talcum Powder Tin 6¼" x 9¼"

MS-340 W. F. Cody Paper
23" x 29"

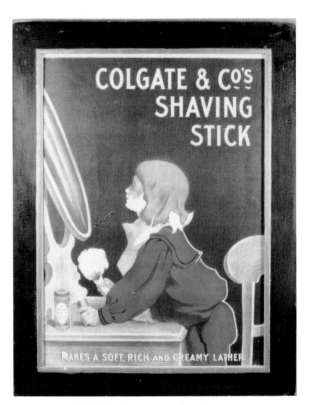

MS-341 Colgate & Co. Paper
15" x 20"

MS-342 Columbia Bicycle Paper 19" x 24"

MS-348 Crosman Bros. Seeds Paper
21" x 28"

MS-349 Crosman Bros. Seeds
Paper 20" x 26"

MS-351 Crystal Springs Dairy Farm
Oil on Canvas 60" x 40"

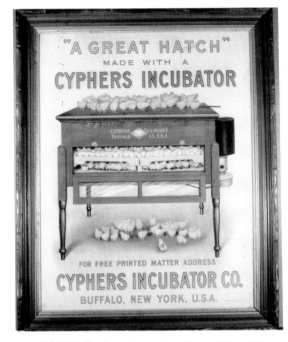

MS-353 Cyphers Incubator Paper 24" x 30"

MS-354 Danfort Chemical Co. Tin 6½" x 9½"

MS-355 Davis Sewing Machine Co.
Paper 20" x 25"

MS-356 Hiram W. Davis & Co. Reverse on Glass 28" x 18"

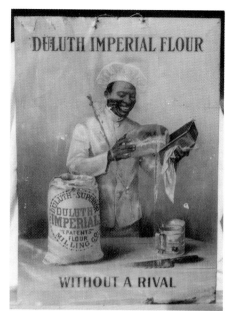

MS-357 Deluth Imperial Flour Tin

MS-361 Diamond Dyes Tin 17" x 11¼"

MS-363 Dr. Pepper Paper

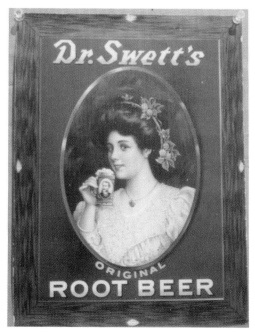

MS-364 Dr. Sweet's Root Beer Cardboard

MS-366 Duxbax Tin Self Framed
15½" x 19½"

MS-368 Edison Mazda Lamps Tin
Two Sided 19" x 23"

MS-369 Chas. Ehlermann Hop & Malt Co. Tin

MS-371 Elgin Watches Wood-Decal

MS-372 Elgin Watches Paper 17" x 24½"

MS-374 Empire Cream Separator
Co. 1910 Calendar

MS-379 Fahy's Watch Case
Paper 12½" x 27"

MS-396 Frostlene Embossed Tin
27" x 19¼"

MS-391 Florence Brushes Paper
12" x 28"

MS-392 Florida Water Paper 14½" x 18½"

MS-383 Fairy Soap Cardboard
Stand-up

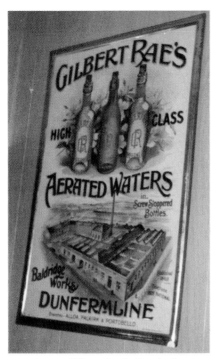

MS-398 Gilbert Rae's Aerated
Waters Embossed Tin
19½" x 28"

MS-399 Gladiator Cycles Automobiles
Paper 16" x 21"

MS-400 Gold Dust
Tin 25½" x 27½"

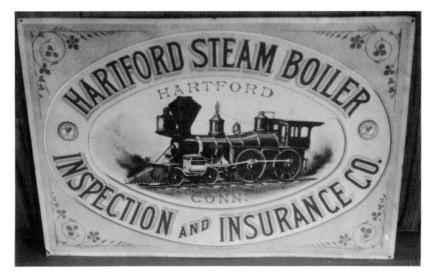

MS-416 Hartford Steam Boiler Tin 20" x 14"

MS-405 Gaudy & Kent Paper 19" x 25"

MS-415 Hartford Fire Insur.
Metal Side Mount 16" x 27"

MS-417 Hecker's Buckwheat Paper 29" x 42"

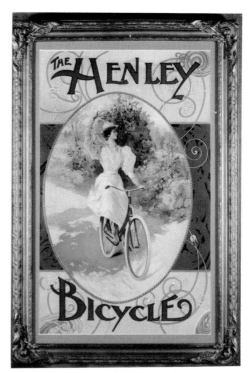

MS-419 Henley Bicycle Paper
13" x 20½"

MS-420 Herald Ranges & Heaters

MS-421 Hickory Garters Wood

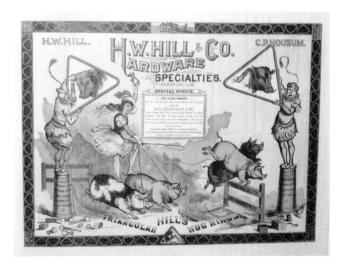

MS-422 H.W. Hill & Co. Paper

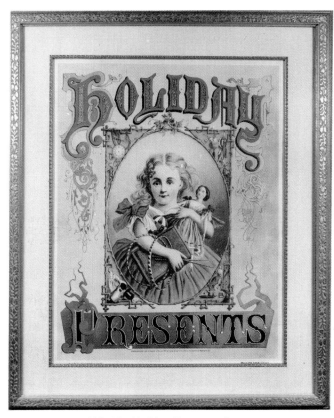

MS-425 Holiday Presents Paper
Date 1871 16" x 20"

MS-426 Hood & Conklin Co. Paper

MS-430 Jos. Hubbard &
Son Paper 15" x 24"

MS-423 Hires Card-
board Stand-up 60"

MS-427 Hood's Ice Cream Metal
Side Mount 21½" x 19¼"

MS-429 Hoyt's German Cologne Tin
23" x 31"

MS-438 Jewett & Root Paper 19" x 25"

MS-448 Kellogg's Corn Flakes Metal Side Mount
13½" x 19½"

MS-450 Keystone Varnish Co.
Tin-Die Cut 9" x 14"

MS-451 Kibbe Chocolates Reverse on Glass 23" x 8½"

MS-454 Kodak Film Porcelain

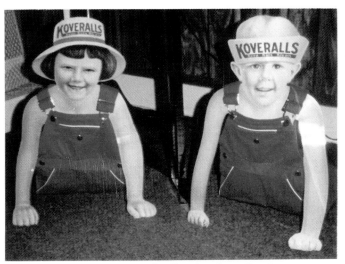

MS-455 Koveralls Tin Die Cut Store Displays

MS-464 Liberty Bell Jelly
Cardboard 12" x 15"

MS-466 E.H. Light's Harness Oil Wood-Two Sided 39" x 22"

MS-468 Lipton's Teas Cardboard 16" x 22"

MS-471 Albert Lorsch Co. Importers
Cardboard 15" x 20½"

MS-474 Lucas Paint Metal Die Cut
26" x 18"

MS-476 Macy's & Co. Paper 43" x 32"

MS-478 Marathon Tires Tin Date 1915
16¾" x 22¾"

MS-479 Mason & Hamlin Organs Paper 24" x 24"

MS-482 Mathushek Pianos Reverse on Glass 16" x 4"

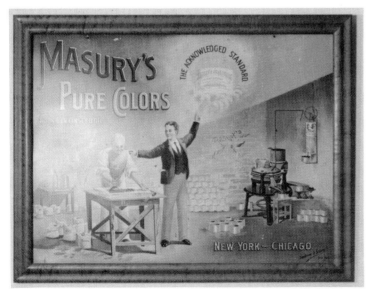

MS-481 Masury's Paint Tin 24" x 18"

MS-488 Monarch Poultry
Feeds Wood 34" x 22"

MS-489 Monitor Stoves
& Ranges Porcelain
Corner Sign 24" x 16"

MS-491 Munsing Wear Metal Die Cut 24" x 16"

MS-496 Matwick Electric Co. Reverse on Glass

MS-505 None Such Mince Meat
Tin 20" x 28"

MS-516 Oliver Chilled Plow Paper

MS-500 New Home Sewing Machine Paper 22" x 27"

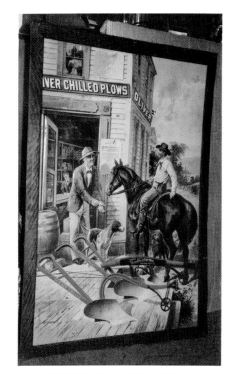

MS-517 Oliver Chilled Plow
Embossed Tin 24" x 30"

MS-519 Orange Crush
Cardboard 12" x 17"

MS-518 Orange Crush
Cardboard 11" x 18"

MS-521 Orient Insurance Tin 20" x 14"

73

MS-522 OxBreeches Embossed Tin 20" x 14"

MS-526 Pepsi Cola Tin 23" x 11½"

MS-524 Peerless Rubber Manufacturing Co.
Paper 21" x 30"

MS-534 Pierce Cycles Paper 42" x 84"

MS-527 Pepsi Cola
Celluloid Over Tin
5¼" x 12¼"

MS-533 Pevely Milk Porcelain

MS-535 F.J. Pike Signs Wood-Gold Leaf
38" x 23"

MS-540 Primley's Chewing Gum Embossed Tin
14" x 20"

MS-542 Pureoxia Ginger Ale
Paper 13½" x 17"

MS-548 Red Seal Dry
Battery Porcelain

MS-544 Quaker Oats Paper 26" x 52"

MS-549 Reid's Flower Seeds Paper 17" x 24"

MS-554 Rub-No-More Washing Powder Canvas
32½" x 29¼"

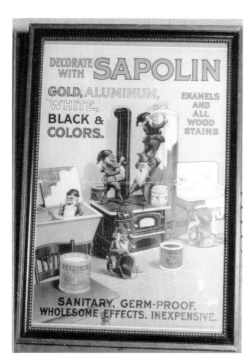

MS-557 Sapolin

MS-555 Runkel Brothers Cocoa Tin 14" x 20"

MS-558 Satan-et Metal Side Mount Die-Cut 20" x 12"

MS-559 Scandinavian-American Line Tin

MS-562 J.S. Sedwick Carriages Paper 16" x 13½"

MS-560 Schrofft's
Chocolates Tin Side Mount
23½" x 23"

MS-564 Selz Shoes Tin

MS-566 Sentenne & Green (Signmakers) Tin

MS-571 Smith American Organ Paper 31" x 22"

MS-574 Solar Tip Shoes Paper 14" x 24"

MS-575 Sozodont Dentifrice Embossed Tin 22" x 16"

MS-577 Squire's Tin Self Framed 19½" x 23½"

MS-578 Standard Bottling & Extract Co.
Celluloid 6"

MS-579 Standard Shirts Paper 20" x 28"

MS-580 Star Soap

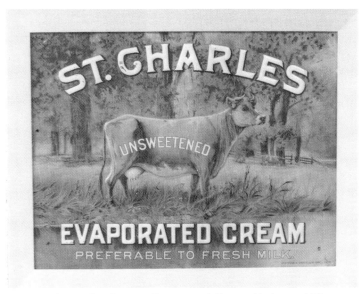

MS-582 St. Charles Evaporated Cream Embossed Tin
21½" x 27"

MS-581 Star Soap Paper 20" x 29"

MS-583 Sterling Stoves Ranges
Porcelain Corner Sign

MS-585 Stickney & Poor Paper 14½" x 26"

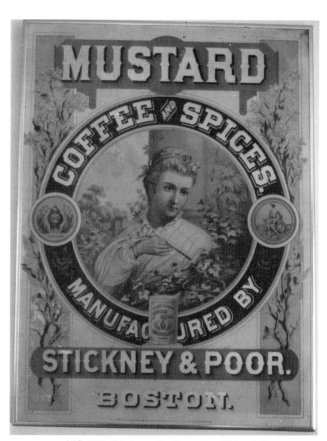

MS-586 Stickney & Poor Tin 18" x 24"

MS-587 Stillson Wrench 12" x 16"
Die Cut Tin 2 Sided

MS-592 Tanglefoot Cardboard 12" x 21"

MS-593 Telegram & Providence Newspaper Paper 18" x 22"

MS-597 Ti-Conder-Oga Paper

MS-600 United Shirt & Collar
Co. Tin 12" x 18"

MS-598 Tuft's Arctic Soda Water Paper 20" x 14"

MS-602 U.S.G. Harness Oil
Embossed Tin-Wood 20" x 30"

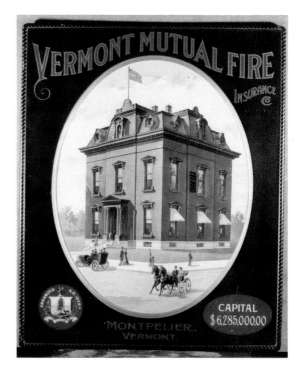

MS-605 Vermont Mutual Fire Insurance Tin 20" x 24"

MS-606 Voigt Milling Co. Cardboard

MS-607 Walk Over Shoes
Metal Side Mount
13½" x 19½"

MS-610 Warrior Mower Co. Paper

MS-609 C.C. Warren & Co. Tin 19¼" x 13¼"

MS-611 Waterman's Pens Tin

MS-612 W.B. Corsets Cardboard 19" x 19"

MS-617 Wertheimer & Co's Paper
18½" x 23½"

MS-616 Well's Richardson & Co's Paper 20" x 26"

MS-618 Western Union Lobby Lamp
16½" x 26¼"

MS-621 Willimantic Spool Cotton Paper 24" x 20"

MS-622 Wilson Sewing Machine Co.
Paper 19" x 23"

MS-631 Wrigley's Gum Cardboard 16½" x 22"

MS-629 Dwinell Wright & Co's
Tin 14" x 20"

MS-626 Wood Taber & Morse's
Paper 28" x 22"

TRAYS

TR-212 Akron Brewing Co. 12"

TR-213 Akron Brewing Co. 14" x 16"

TR-215 August Bohn Brewery 14" x 16"

TR-216 Bartels Brewing Co. 12"

TR-217 Bartholomay Porcelain 12"

TR-218 Belmont Brewing Co. 12"

TR-219 Berkshire Brewery Assoc.
16½" x 13½"

TR-220 Peter Breidt Brewing Co. 13" x 16"

TR-221 Bucyrus Brewing Co. 13"

TR-222 Burkhardt's Brewing Co. 13" x 10"

TR-223 Casey & Kelly Brewery 13"

TR-224 Christ. Diehl Brewing 12"

TR-225 Christo Ginger Ale 13"

TR-226 City Brewery 14" x 16"

TR-227 H. Clausen & Son Brewing Co.
Porcelain and Brass 16"

TR-229 Cleveland Sandusky Brewing Co. 13"

TR-231 Consumers Brewing Co. 16" x 13"

TR-232 Crockery City Beer 13"

TR-233 J.H. Cutter Whiskey 17" x 14"

TR-234 Dawson's Porcelain 12"

TR-235 Eagle Brewing Co. Porcelain 13" x 16"

TR-236 Ebling Brewing Co. 13" x 16"

TR-237 Emmerling Brewing Co. 13" x 10"

TR-238 Erie Brewing Co. 14" x 16"

TR-240 Foss-Schneider Brewing Co. 14" x 16"

TR-244 L. Hoster Brewing Co. 13" x 16"

TR-242 Fruit Syrups 10½" x 14"

TR-243 Glennon's Beer 13" x 13"

TR-245 Hubert Fischer Brewery Porcelain 12"

TR-246 Huebner Brewing Co. 12"

TR-249 Iroquois Brewery 12"

TR-251 Leisey Brewing Co. 12" x 15"

TR-254 Narragansett Porcelain 12"

TR-255 Oneida Brewing Co. Porcelain 12"

TR-257 Ruhstaller's Gilt Edge 13¼" x 13¼"

TR-258 L. Schlather Brewing Porcelain & Brass 12"

TR-259 L. Schlather Nickel Plated 12"

TR-260 Frank X. Schwab Co.

TR-262 Spray Beer Porcelain 12"

TR-263 Star Brewing Co 13"

TR-264 Stoll Brewing Co. Porcelain 12"

TR-265 Suffolk Brewing Co. 12"

TR-266 Sunrise Beer 12"

TR-268 Walsh & Co. Whiskey 10½" x 13¼"

MO-1 Moxie Cardboard
3-D Bottle Display
10" x 28" x 5"

MO-2 Moxie Cardboard Die Cut 16½" x 16"

MO-3 Moxie Cardboard Stand-Up 24" x 38"

MO-4 Moxie Cardboard Stand-Up 28" x 39"

MO-5 Moxie Cardboard Stand-Up
23" x 38"

MO-6 Moxie Cardboard Stand-Up

MO-7 Moxie Cardboard Stand-Up 6" x 16"

MO-8 Moxie Embossed Tin 27" x 19"

MO-9 Moxie
Embossed Tin
19" x 54"

MO-10 Metal Cooler 22" x 31" x 33"

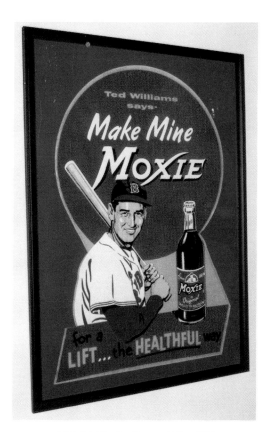

MO-11 Moxie Paper 21" x 32"

MO-12 Moxie Ponies Cigar Box

99

MO-13 Reverse
Glass 9" x 5"

MO-14 Moxie Reverse
Glass Over Wood
8" x 10"

MO-15 Reverse Glass Serving
Tray 10"

MO-16 Moxie Tin
42" x 15"

MO-20 Moxie Tin
Thermometer 10" x 25"

MO-18 Moxie Tin
Die Cut 6"

MO-17 Moxie
Tin Over Wood
Thermometer
12" x 39"

MO-19 Moxie Tin Over Cardboard
9" x 6½"

MO-21 Moxie Tin Thermometer
12½" x 12½"

MO-23 Moxie Wood
Statue 33"

MO-22 Moxie
Tin Thermo-
meter 10" x 25"

MO-24 Moxie Tin 14" x 18"

MO-25 Moxie Embossed Tin 14" x 8"

MO-26 Moxie Cardboard Stand-up 39" x 28"

MO-27 Moxie Cardboard 36" x 24"

MO-29 Moxie Embossed Tin 28" x 24"

MO-28 Moxie Embossed Tin 30" x 24"

HEINZ FOOD PRODUCTS CONTAINERS

HF-1 Heinz Apple Butter
Crockery 8½"

HF-2 Heinz Apple Butter
Crockery 5¾"

HF-3 Heinz Appler Butter
Crockery 5¼"

HF-4 Heinz Apple
Butter 8"

HF-5 Heinz's Aromatic
Malt Vinegar Crockery
11½"

HF-6 Heinz Cran-
berry Sauce
Crockery 8½"

HF-7 Heinz Damson Pre-
serves Tin 6½" x 4½"

HF-8 Heinz Dill
Vinegar 13½"

HF-9 Heinz Hotel Catsup
Crockery 9½"

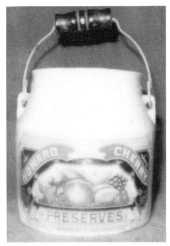

HF-10 Heinz Howard
Cherry Preserves Crockery
5"

HF-11 Heinz Mince Meat
Wood 12" x 12"

HF-12 Heinz Mince
Meat Crockery 6½"

HF-12A Heinz
Mixed Pickles
11¾"

HF-13 Heinz Mus-
tard Crockery 6"

HF-14 Heinz Peach Pre-
serves Crockery 9½"

HF-15 Heinz Preserved Black-
berries Crockery 8"

HF-16 Heinz Preserved
Cherries Wood 10" x 9¾"

HF-17 Heinz Pre-
served Cherries
Crockery 5¾"

HF-18 Heinz Preserved
Pineapple Crockery 5"

HF-19 Heinz Preser-
ved Tomatoes Crockery
5"

HF-21 Heinz Quince
Jelly Tin 5" x 10"

HF-20 Heinz Quince Jelly
Crockery 8"

HF-22 Heinz Quince
Preserves Crockery 6"

HF-23 Heinz Raspberry
Jelly Crockery 5¾"

HF-24 Heinz Red Raspberries
Wood 8½" x 7¼"

HF-25 Heinz
Tomato Marma-
lade Tin 6" x 7"

HF-26 Heinz
Vinegar 13½"

HF-27 Heinz Vinegar
Crockery 8"

HF-28 Heinz Vinegar
11½"

MISCELLANEOUS ITEMS

M-206 Walter Baker & Co. China Pot 10" Cocoa Mugs

M-205 American Gold Eagle Coffee
Paper Mache

M-207 Walter Baker & Co,. China Cocoa Pots 8" 10" 10"

M-213 Buster Brown Shoes Metal
Shoe Rack 15" x 8"

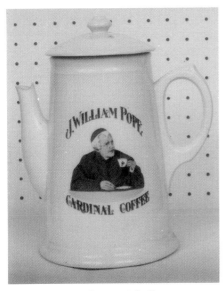

M-217 Cardinal Coffee

M-228 Lutted
Cough Drop Glass
Jar 11"

M-220 Diamond Dyes Cabinet 24" x 10" x 31"

M-222 Tony Faust's Saloon Token
Dispenser Date 1890 Wood
12¹₂" x 15"

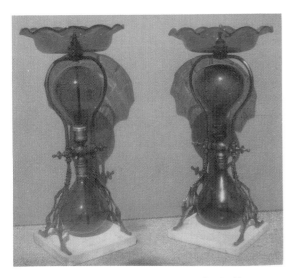

M-223 Fountain Displays Tuft's Soda Fountain Co. 21" high 8" base

M-231 Owl Choco-
late Co. Glass Jar 15½"

M-233 Pony Stockings Paper Mache
24½" x 23½"

M-234 Quaker Oats
Paper Mache 54"

M-235 Revolving Display
Case 32 Bins Date 1894 41"

M-239 String & Paper Dispenser
Cast Iron 8" x 18" x 22"

M-240 Taylor's Candy Cardboard Box

GP-1 Adams
Tutti-Frutti Gum
Wood & Porcelain
10" x 10" x 32"

GP-2 Brouse's
Peerless Fruit Gum
Wood & Porcelain
10" x 10" x 30"

GP-3 Chiclets-Stoll-
werck Chocolates
Wood & Porcelain
10" x 9½" x 32"

GP-13 Peanut Ven-
der Wood & Iron
10" x 10" x 28"

GP-16 Pulvers
Kola-Pepsi
Embossed Tin
10" x 5" x 24"

GP-17 Tutti Frutti Gum
Iron 7" x 17" x 6"

GP-6 Loop the Loop Gum Iron 11½" x 7" x 18"

GP-19 Vending Figure
Zinc 7" x 8" x 36"

GP-20 Walter
Baker & Co.
Wood &
Porcelain
9½" x 9" x 32"

COCA-COLA ITEMS

CC-35 Coca-Cola Cardboard Bi-Fold 50" x 34"

CC-34 Coca Cola Cardboard
21" x 38"

CC-36 Coca Cola Cardboard 11" x 22"

GUN POWDER ADVERTISING

GUN-2 Austin Powder Co. Paper Calendar
1900 21½" x 38"

GUN-6 Colt Revolvers

GUN-7 E.I. Dupont DeNemours & Co. Metal 24" x 36"

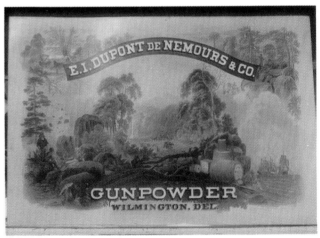

GUN-8 E.I. Dupont Tin 20" x 14"

GUN-11 Hazard Powder Co. Tin 34" x 26"

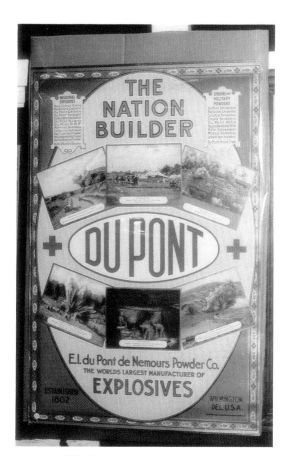

GUN-9 DuPont Powder Paper

GUN-14 King Powder Co. "Quick Shot"
Paper & Mat 25" x 31½"

GUN-13 Ithaga Guns Embossed Tin 6½" x 13½"

CLOCKS

CL-1 Belle Bourbon Metal Clock

CL-2 Bull Durham 6"

CL-3 Chief Bonus Tea
(Baird Clock)

CL-4 Coca-Cola Clock
Neon-Porcelain Bottle

CL-5 Erie Hollow Ware
Heavy Metal 10" x 14" x 2½"

Cl-6 Fitu Corset
40"

CL-7 Garfield Tea
(Baird Clock)

CL-13 Reed's Tonic 25"

CL-14 Sidney Advertising Clock Date
1888 28" x 68"

Bottom of CL-14

MTC-14 Norton Bros. Spice Pagoda-Tin 41"

MTC-19A Richardson's
Cough Drops 8" x 5" x 5"

TOBACCO CUTTERS & LIGHTERS

TCU-35 Base-
ball Batter Cigar
Lighter Iron
6" x 6" x 12"

TCU-40 Cigar Cutter & Lighter
Iron 13½" x 18"

TCU-69 M. Thomas
Cigar Cutter & Lighter
Iron 6" x 10" x 14"

BREWERY SIGNS

BS-138 Alamo Girl (Lone Star) Paper 21½" x 25½"

BS-139 Alamo Girl (Lone Star) Paper 20" x 25¾"

BS-144 Anheuser-Busch Heavy Cardboard
38½" x 19½"

BS-140 Alamo Girl (Lone Star) Tin 16½" x 22"

BS-145 Ashland Brewing Co. Tin
24" x 20"

BS-147 P. Barbey & Son Brewers Paper
15½" x 21½"

BS-149 Magnus Beck Brewing Co. Cardboard
21½" x 25"

BS-152 Beverwyck Irish Cream
Ale Tin 11" x 11"

BS-155 Broadway Lager Reverse on Glass 24" x 35"

BS-158 Budweiser Wood
30" x 20"

BS-156 Bruckmann Co.
Brewers Cloth Tire
Cover

BS-159 Budweiser Paper 23" x 36"

BS-160 Budweiser Tin Self Framed 26" x 37"

BS-168 Dobler Brewing Co. Reverse on Glass 35" x 23"

BS-171 DuBoise Beer Milk Glass
Corner Sign

BS-175 Erie Brewing Co. Tin

BS-176 Evansville Brewery Paper
22" x 16½"

BS-177 Frank Fehr Brewing Co. Tin Sel Framed
39½" x 27½"

BS-179 M.D. Goetz Brewing Co. Tin
28½" x 22½"

BS-180 Grand Prize Beer Cardboard & paper mache
16" x 17½"

BS-181 Gund's Beer Tin

BS-183 Harvard Brewing Co. Tin 40" x 28"

BS-187 Hoster's Brewing Co.
Tin 24"

BS-190 Indianapolis Brewing Co. Paper
29½" x 37½"

BS-194 Frank Jones Brewing Co. Tin 43" x 29"

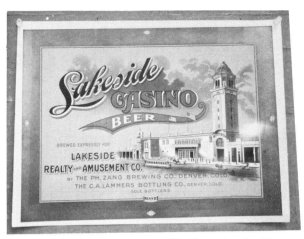

BS-204 Lakeside Casino Beer Ph. Zang Brewing Co.
Paper

BS-211 Loyalhanna Brewing Co.

BS-209 Lemp Brewery Tin Die Cut (Sits
on edge of shelf)
6¼" x 19½"

BS-210 Lone Star Brewing
Embossed Cardboard
6" x 28"

BS-217 Moerlein Beer Canvass 15¾" x 11¾"

BS-218 Moerlein's Beer Heavy
Paper 14¼" x 20"

BS-221 Orange County
Brewery Paper Calendar-
Date 1910 28" x 15"

BS-222 Pabst
Beer Wood
14" x 33"

BS-223 Pabst Brewing Co. Paper 32" x 24"

BS-227 Rainier Brewing Paper Date
1910 18" x 29"

BS-225 Phoenix Brewery Tin
20" x 24"

BS-228 Renner Brewery
Paper 14¼" x 20"

BS-230 Rochester Brewing
Co. Metal 28" x 20"

BS-237 Springfield Brewing
Company Paper 20" x 26¼"

BS-238 Standard Brew-
ing Co. Wood

BS-239 Texas Brewing Co. Tin Self Framed
22½" x 28½"

BS-240 Toby All Tin 21" x 14¾"

BS-242 Valley Brew Tin 13½"

BS-243 John Walter & Co. Milk Glass
Corner Sign 15¼" x 20¼"

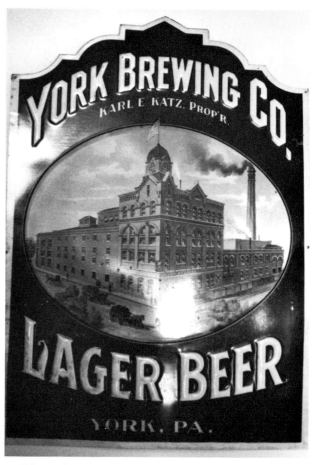

BS-245 York Brewing Co. Embossed Tin 20" x 28"

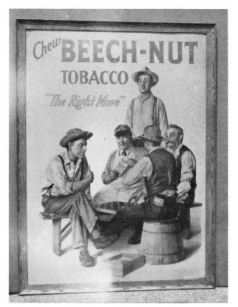

TS-165 Beech Nut Tobacco Cardboard 44½" x 33½"

TS-166 Between The Acts
Paper 21" x 14"

TS-167 "Black Cat" Cigarettes Porcelain
24" x 36"

TS-169 Blackwell's Durham Tobacco Paper 10" x 13"

TS-171 Brucker & Boghien Tin

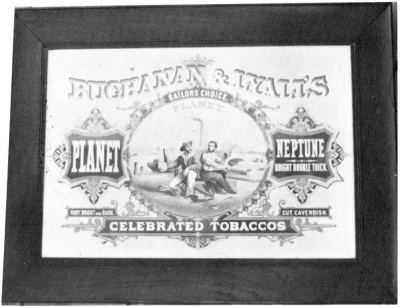

TS-172 Buchanan & Lyall's Tobacco Paper 21" x 14"

TS-173 Buck Cigars
Tin 10¼" x 12½"

TS-174 Robert Burns Milk Glass
Corner Sign 22" x 17½"

TS-177 Cortez Cigars Tin
11¾" x 16¼"

TS-178 Cubanola Cigar Cardboard 22½" x 24¼"

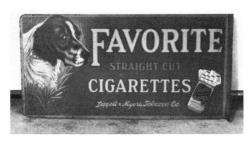

TS-179 Favorite Cigarettes Metal Side
Mount 18" x 9"

TS-182 Anna Held Cigars Cardboard 36" x 15"

TS-188 London Life Cigarettes Porcelain Side Mount 18" x 15½"

TS-192 Lucky Strike Cardboard
1932 34¼" x 25½"

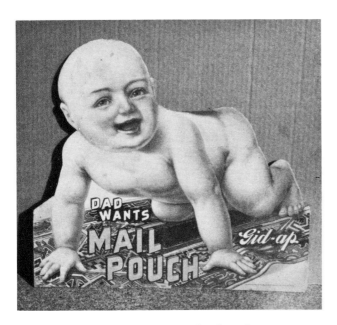

TS-193 Mail Pouch Cardboard
Stand Up 17½" x 15½"

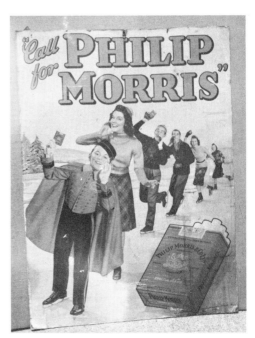

TS-197 Philip Morris Cardboard
31" x 42"

TS-198 Napoleon Cigars Embossed
Tin 20"

TS-200 Gail & Ax Navy Paper 30" x 23"

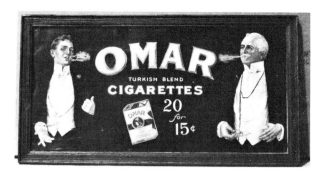

TS-206 Omar Cigarettes Tin 23" x 11"

TS-201 Newsboy Plug Tobacco
Cardboard 10" x 16¼"

TS-202 Newsboy Plug Tobacco
Paper 10" x 16¼"

TS-210 Pickett Tobacco Warehouse Paper 17" x 22"

TS-212 Punch & Judy Tobacco Paper
10" x 13"

TS-215 John Ruskin Cigar
Cardboard

TS-218 Sunny Side Tobacco Paper

TS-219 Sunshine Cigar-
ettes Tin 13" x 17"

TS-220 Tomahawk Plug Cardboard
25" x 17"

TS-223 Velvet Tobacco Porcelain 39" x 12"

MDS-2 Antikamnia Tablets 1908
Calendar Heavy Cardboard
7¾" x 10"

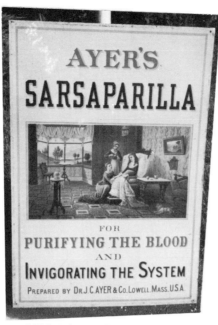

MDS-7 Ayer's Sarsaparilla Tin
14" x 20"

MDS-16 Dr. Caldwell's Syrup Pepsin
Cardboard 21" x 11"

MDS-17 Dr. Caldwell's Syrup Pepsin
Cardboard 12¾" x 10¾"

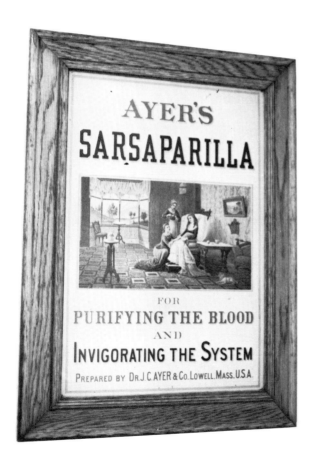

MDS-10 Ayer's Sarsaparilla Tin 14" x 20"

MDS-19 Dr. W.B. Caldwell
Cardboard Stand Up
15" x 21¾"

MDS-20 Dr. W.B. Caldwell's
Cardboard Stand Up
15¼" x 21¾"

MDS-21 Cascasweet Paper
20¾" x 19¼"

MDS-23 Dr. A.C. Daniels Paper 21" x 27"

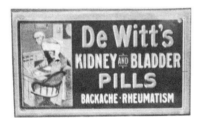

MDS-25 DeWitt's Paper
18¼" x 10¼"

MDS-26 Dr. Drakes
Croup Remedy Card-
board Hanger
7¾" x 11"

MDS-27 Father John's Medicine Cardboard Mechanical Clock Work Mechanism 40" x 39"

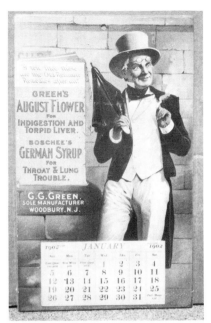

MDS-30 Green's August Flower
Cardboard Calendar 1902
9¾" x 15¾"

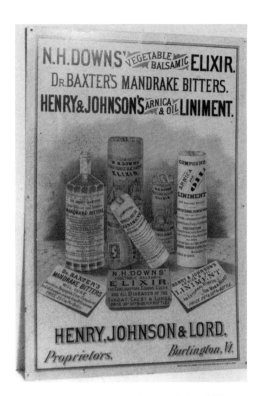

MDS-33 Henry Johnson & Lord Tin
14" x 20"

MDS-31 Green's August Flower Paper
8" x 10"

MDS-37 Kendall's Spavin Cure
Paper 26" x 21¼"

MDS-36 Hoods Sarsaparilla Heavy
Cardboard 29½" x 42¼"

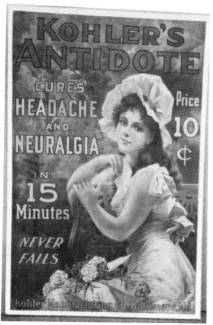

MDS-38 Kohler's Antidote Cardboard 42" x 28"

MDS-40 Lash's Bitters Cardboard
13¾" x 9¼"

MDS-41A Our Standard Remedy Cardboard
14" x 10"

MDS-41 Moxie Nerve Food Cardboard 27½" x 21"

MDS-43 Pepsinic Seltzer Cardboard Metal
Edge 21" x 10"

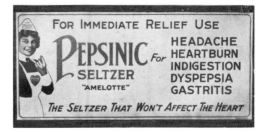

MDS-42 Pe-Ru-Na Tonic Cardboard
19½" x 32"

MDS-44 Peruvian Syrup Wistar's Balsam
Dr. H. Anders Grace's Salve Reverse on Glass
21½" x 18"

MDS-45 Dr. Pierce's
Cardboard 10¾" x 13¼"

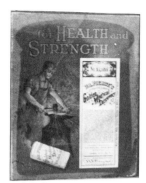

MDS-46 Dr. Pierce's
Cardboard 10¾" x 13¼"

MDS-47 Dr. Pierce's
Cardboard 10¾" x 13¼"

MDS-48 Dr. Pierce's
Cardboard 10¾" x 13¼"

MDS-56 Warner's Log
Cabin Paper 12½" x 27½"

MDS-52 Schenck's Mandrake Pills Tin 22" x 30"

MDS-58 Warner's Safe
Yeast Tippecanoe Bitters
Paper 29½" x 15"

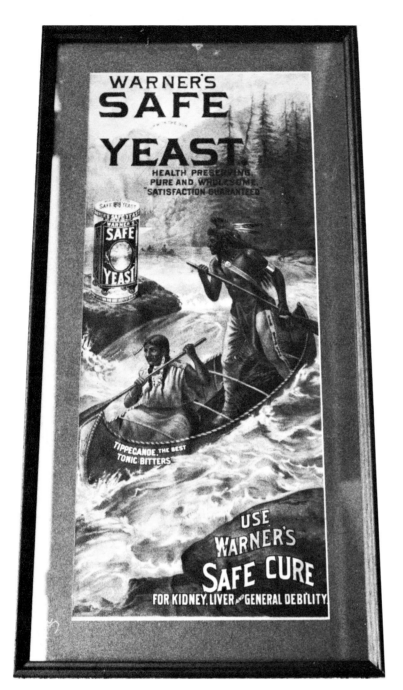

MDS-57 Warner's Safe Yeast Paper 12" x 28"

MDS-60 Warner's Safe
Yeast Paper

MDS-61 Dr. E.L.
Welbourn's Medicine
Metal Side Mount
12¾" x 6¼"

WS-85 Brown Forman Co. Distillers Tin Wood Frame 35" x 27½"

WS-87 Fred Crickson's Whiskey Tin Self Framed
38½" x 23"

WS-90 El Bart Dry Gin Tin 9¼" x 13¼"

WS-91 Frerker Bros. & Co. Tin Self Framed 33½" x 23"

WS-95 Kris Kringle Rye Paper 18½" x 23½"

WS-97 Meadville Rye Whiskey Tin
33" x 43"

WS-102 Morrin Powers Co. Paper 27½" x 22½"

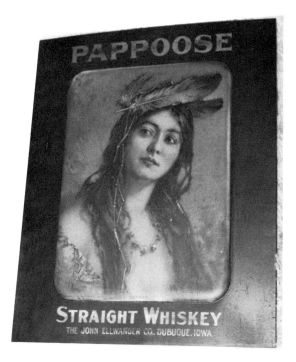

WS-100 Pappoose Whiskey Tin Self Framed
12" x 14½"

WS-103 Pride of Kentucky Whiskey Paper
50" x 40"

MA-1 Apollo Club Cardboard 14" x 22"

MA-2 Ardison's Cardboard 14" x 22"

MA-3 Ardison's Cardboard 14" x 22"

MA-4 Ardison's Cardboard 14" x 22"

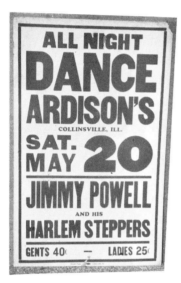

MA-5 Ardison's Cardboard 14" x 22"

MA-6 Ardison's Cardboard 14" x 22"

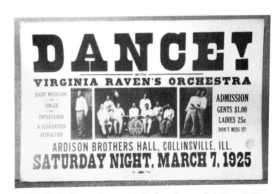

MA-7 Ardison Bros. Hall Cardboard 14" x 22"

MA-8 Louis Armstrong Cardboard 14" x 22¼" Orig. Art Work

MA-9 Tex Beneke Orig. Art Work

MA-10 Bluebird Records Erskine Hawkins Cardboard 23¾" x 17¾"

MA-11 Bluebird Records Pastor Cardboard 23¾" x 17¾"

MA-12 Bluebird Records Dinah Shore Cardboard 23¾" x 17¾"

MA-13 Brookside Ballroom Fenton Bros. Cardboard 14" x 22"

MA-14 Brookside Ballroom D. McGinley Orch. Cardboard 14" x 22"

MA-15 Brookside Ballroom Cardboard 14" x 22"

MA-16 Brookside Park Cardboard 14" x 22"

MA-17 Casino Ball Room Metal Side Mount (Two Sided) 25¾" x 19¼"

MA-18 Capitol Records Wood 28"

MA-19 Chesterfield Cardboard 21" x 22"

MA-20 Chesterfield Cardboard 21" x 22"

MA-21 Columbia Grafonola Mechanical Cardboard Fan 8"

MA-22 Columbia Masterworks
Cardboard 16¼" x 22"

MA-23 Columbia Masterworks
Cardboard 17" x 22"

MA-24 Columbia Masterworks
Cardboard 17" x 22"

MA-25 Columbia Records
Cardboard 20¾" x 13½"

MA-26 Columbia Records Porcelain 28"

MA-27 Colum-
bia Records
Metal 61" x 18"

MA-28 Columbia Records
Cardboard 16" x 22"

MA-29 Columbia Records
Cardboard 16" x 22"

MA-30 Columbia Records Cardboard 24½" x 19"

MA-31 Columbia Records Cardboard 16" x 22"

MA-32 Columbia Records Cardboard 16" x 22"

MA-33 Columbia Records Cardboard Stand Up 6½" x 11¾"

MA-34 Columbia Records Cardboard 16" x 22"

MA-35 Columbia Records Cardboard 16" x 22"

MA-36 Columbia Records Cardboard 16" x 22"

MA-37 Columbia Records Cardboard Stand Up 16" x 22"

MA-38 Columbia Records Cardboard 16" x 22"

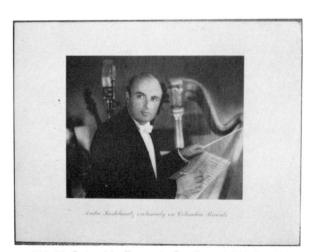

MA-39 Columbia Records Cardboard 24½" x 19"

MA-40 Columbia Records Cardboard 16" x 22"

MA-41 Columbia Records Cardboard 6½" x 11¾"

MA-42 Columbia Records Cardboard 16" x 22"

MA-43 Columbia Records Cardboard 16" x 22"

MA-44 Columbia Records Cardboard 24½" x 19"

MA-45 Columbia Records Cardboard 24½" x 19"

MA-46 Columbia Records Cardboard 24½" x 19"

MA-47 Columbia Records Cardboard 24½" x 19"

MA-48 Columbia Records Cardboard 24½" x 19"

MA-49 Columbia Records Cardboard 24½" x 19"

MA-50 Columbia Records Cardboard 16" x 22"

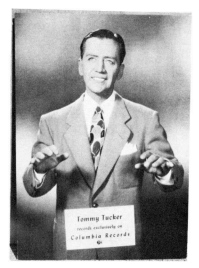

MA-51 Columbia Records Cardboard 16" x 22"

MA-52 Columbia Records Cardboard 24½" x 19"

MA-53 Columbia Records Cardboard 16" x 22"

MA-55 Discos Victor Porcelain
19¾"

MA-57 Eagle Brand Musical String Case
Metal 17" x 7¾" x 12½"

MA-54 Coronas Wood Cigar Box Signed by Paul
Whiteman and Orchestra Dated 3-1-28
9¼" x 6¼" x 2½" RARE

MA-56 Jimmy Dorsey Cardboard
27½" x 22"

MA-58 Ray Eberle Heavy Cardboard
40" x 60"

MA-59 Duke Ellington Orig. Art
work Cardboard 22" x 28"

MA-60 Ferrante & Teicher Heavy
Cardboard 40" x 60"

MA-61 Fitch's Shampoo Cardboard 24" x 36¾"

MA-62 General Electric Cardboard Stand Up
25" x 12¾"

MA-63 Golden Gate Palace
Cardboard 14" x 22"

MA-64 Glen Gray Cardboard
27½" x 22"

MA-65 Mal Hallett Card-
board 14" x 22"

MA-66 Lionel Hampton Cardboard
20" x 30" Wood & Metal Frame

MA-67 Lionel Hampton Paper
16½" x 21¼"

MA-68 W.C. Handy Orig.
Art Work Cardboard
14¼" x 22"

MA-69 Erskine Hawkins Orig.
Artwork Cardboard 22" x 28"

MA-70 J.C. Haynes & Co. Bay State
Banjos Cardboard 15" x 10½"

MA-71 J.C. Haynes & Co. Cardboard
15" x 10½"

MA-72 J.C. Haynes & Co. Cardboard
15" x 10½"

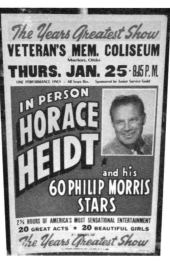

MA-73 Horace Heidt Card-
board 22" x 14"

MA-74 Hot Lips Page Card-
board 14" x 22"

MA-75 Jeter-Pillars Orig.
Art Work Cardboard 22" x 28¼"

MA-76 Buddy Johnson Orig. Art
Work Cardboard 19" x 24"

MA-77 Eddie Johnson Orig. Art Work
Cardboard 17" x 22"

MA-78 G-W-P Jones Music
Co. Porcelain 21" x 14"

MA-79 Louis Jordan Cardboard
18¾" x 14"

MA-80 Keglined Cans Paper 7¾" x 9¾"

MA-81 Lucky Strike Card-
board Stand Up 13" x 25"

MA-82 Jimmie Lunceford Orig. Art Work
Cardboard 17" x 11"

MA-83 Majestic Radio Paper 9½" x 36"

MA-84 Metropolitan Opera Co. Cardboard 27¾" x 12½"

MA-85 Vaughn Monroe Card-
board 27½" x 22"

MA-86 Tony Mottola Card-
board 20" x 27¾"

MA-87 Ozzie Nelson Cardboard
18" x 14"

MA-88 Nipper
Paper Mache 14"

MA-89 Old Gold Cardboard
35" x 26½"

MA-90 Pathe Chalk
Rooster (Base Reads-
No Needles to Change)
23"

MA-91 Pathe' Records Metal Side
Mount 18½" x 13½"

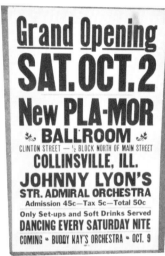

MA-92 Pla-Mor Ballroom
Cardboard 14" x 22"

MA-93 RCA Victor Records
Cardboard 18" x 24"

MA-94 RCA Victor Records
Cardboard 18" x 24"

MA-95 Alvino Rey Cardboard
20" x 27¾"

MA-96 Rhythm Aces Base Drum
27"

MA-97 Rhythm Kings
Megaphone - Holes in
back side for hands
37½"

MA-98 Ring's Talking
Machines Canvas and
Wood Stool 21" x 12" x 11"

MA-99 B.A. Rolfe Lucky Strike
Cardboard 22" x 14"

MA-100 Royal Crown Cola Cardboard
39" x 26¼"

MA-101 Summit Beach Ball-
room Cardboard 15½" x 23½"

MA-102 Sunset Terrace
Cardboard 22" x 14"

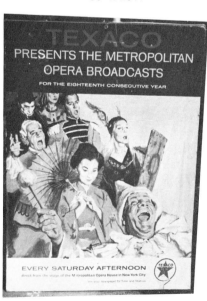

MA-103 Texaco Cardboard
27½" x 20"

MA-104 Three Suns Heavy
Cardboard 40" x 60"

MA-105 Triena Laxa-
tive Cardboard Fan
8¼" x 11¼"

155

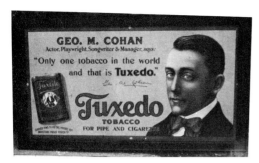

MA-106 Tuxedo Cardboard 21¼" x 11¼"

MA-107 Thos. D. VanOsten Paper
21" x 38"

MA-108 Van Osten & Day Paper
21" x 28"

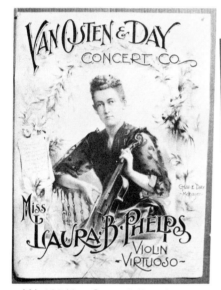

MA-109 Van Osten & Day Paper
21" x 28"

MA-110 Van Osten Paper 21" x 28"

MA-111 Bobby Vinton-Krupa Cardboard 27" x 21"

MA-112 Victor
Records Paper
36" x 13"

MA-113 Victor Records Cardboard 19½" x 10½"

MA-114 Victor Records
Cardboard 15" x 20"

MA-115 Victor Records Cardboard 18" x 24"

MA-116 Victor Records Cardboard 23¾" x 17¾"

MA-117 Victor Records Cardboard 15" x 20"

MA-118 Victor Records Cardboard 15" x 20"

MA-119 Victor Records Cardboard 15" x 20"

MA-120 Victor Records Cardboard 15" x 20"

MA-121 Victor Records Cardboard 20¾" x 11"

MA-122 Victor Records Cardboard 15" x 20"

MA-123 Victor Records Cardboard 15" x 20"

MA-124 Victor Records Cardboard 15" x 20"

MA-125 Victor Records Cardboard 18" x 24"

MA-126 Victor Records Cardboard 18" x 24"

MA-127 Victor Records Cardboard 15" x 20"

MA-128 Victor Records Cardboard 23¾" x 17¾"

MA-129 Victor Records Cardboard 15" x 20"

MA-130 Victor Records Cardboard 15" x 20"

MA-131 Victrola Cardboard Fan 8"

MA-132 Victrola Cardboard 19" x 27¾"

MA-133 Victrola Cardboard Puzzle
8¼"

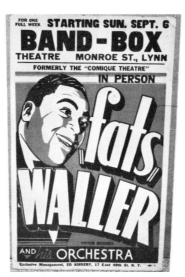

MA-134 Fat's Waller Card-
board 14" x 22"

MA-135 Jimmy Walls
Cardboard 14" x 22"

MA-136 Eddie Cantor Cardboard 21" x 11"

MA-137 Lester Young Orig.
Art Work Cardboard
22" x 28¼"

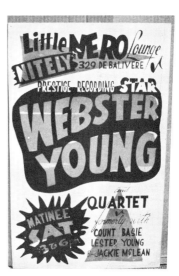

MA-138 Webster Young Cardboard 14¼" x 22"

MA-139 Victrola Cardboard

MA-140 Spike Jones Card-
board Stand Up
13¼" x 25½"

MA-141 Columbia Re-
cords Nelson Eddy
6½" x 12" Cardboard
Stand Up

GUN POWDER ADVERTISING

GUN-1 Austin's Gun Powder Tin 7" x 20"

GUN-3 Austin Powder Co. paper 16½" x 21½"

GUN-4 Black Shells
Cardboard

GUN-5 Colt Paper 19" x 20"

GUN-10 Forehand Revolvers Embossed Tin
13½" x 9½"

GUN-12 Hercules Powder
Co. Paper 15" x 24"

GUN-15 Peters 1907 Calendar 20" x 34½"

GUN-16 Peters Ammunition
Paper 20" x 30"

GUN-17 Peters Ammunition Paper 25½" x 36½"

GUN-18 Peters Cartridge Co. Paper
13½" x 28½"

GUN-19 Peters Shells
Cardboard 13"

GUN-20 Remington Arms Paper
23" x 16"

GUN-21 Remington U.M.C. Metal
Side Mount 7" x 8"

GUN-22 Remington U.M.C.
Cardboard Stand Up 19" x 14½"

GUN-24 Union Metallic Cartridge Co. 57½" x 42¾"
Cardboard

GUN-23 U.M.C. Cartridge Metal Side Mount
18" x 27"

GUN-25 U.S.
Cartridge Card-
board

GUN-26 U.S. Cartridges 1925 Calendar
24½" x 40½"

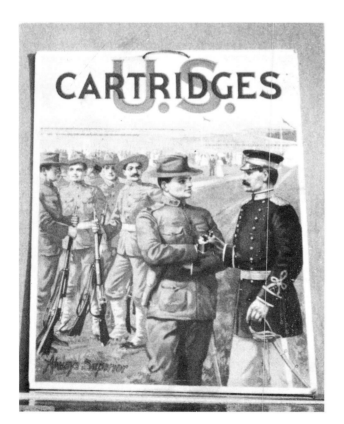

GUN-27 U.S. Cartridges
Cardboard

GUN-28 Western Shot Shells
Cardboard

GUN-29 Winchester Cardboard
8½" x 12½"

GUN-30 Winchester Arms Co.
Paper Calendar 1897

GUN-31 Winchester Arms Co.
Paper Calendar 1898

GUN-32 Winchester Arms Co.
Paper Calendar 1901

GUN-33 Winchester
Repeating Arms Co.
Metal Scale
6" x 8¾" x 8¼"

GUN-34 Winchester Repeating Arms Co. Date 1908
Paper 21" x 29"

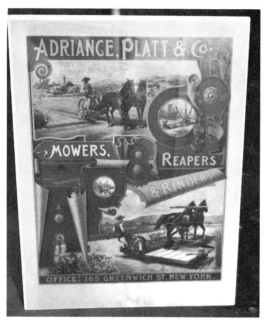

MS-266 Adriance Platt & Co. Paper
28" x 22"

MS-267 Adriance Platt & Co. Paper 28" x 22"

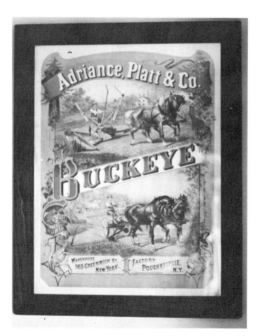

MS-268 Adriance Platt & Co. Paper Date
1872 18½" x 23½"

MS-269 Alta Ginger Ale Tin Self Framed
13¼" x 19¼"

MS-272 American Tissue Mills Cardboard & Tissue Stand-up 19½" x 18¾"

MS-274 Anti-Freeze Cardboard 28" x 25"

MS-275 Argo Salmon
Embossed Tin
9¾" x 13¾"

MS-278 Arrow Shirts Card-
board (Signed Norman Rock-
well) 9¼" x 12¼"

MS-279 Arrow Shirts
Cardboard
9¼" x 12¼"

MS-280 Arrow Shirts Cardboard
(Signed Edward Penfield)
12¾" x 9¾"

MS-282 Aultman, Miller & Co. Paper Date 1872
22" x 28"

MS-283 Aultman & Taylor Machinery Co.
Embossed Tin 14" x 20"

MS-299 Barry Shoe Milk Glass
Corner Sign 18" x 25"

MS-288 Baby Esmond Tin 27¾" x 20"

MS-298 Baronet Biscuit Cardboard 21" x 11"

MS-300 Bartholomew Co. Embossed Tin 7" x 14"

MS-301 Battery Cardboard 38" x 25"

MS-302 Becker's Fishermen's Grain Paper 34" x 28"

MS-303 Beeman's Pepsin
Gum Cardboard 8" x 12"

MS-305 Bemis Brother & Co.
Tin 13¾" x 20"

MS-304 Bee Starch Paper 15" x 23"

MS-308 Big Guy Embossed Tin 19¾" x 6¾"

MS-311 Body & Fender Work Cardboard 38" x 25"

MS-314 Brake Adjustment Cardboard 38" x 25"

MS-315 Brakes Cardboard 28" x 25"

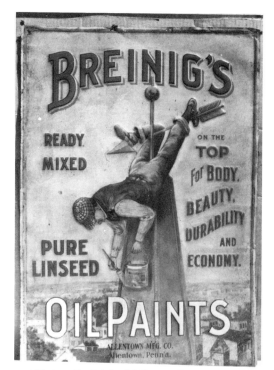

MS-316 Breinig's Oil Paints Embossed Tin

MS-317 Brownie
Chocolate Soda
Cardboard 21" x 60"

MS-320 Buffalo Bill-Pawnee Bill Paper
42½" x 29½"

MS-319 Buckeye Paints Wood

MS-321 Buffalo Bill-Pawnee Bill Iron
Tail Paper 42½" x 29¼"

MS-322 Buffalo Bill Paper 43¾" x 30¾"

MS-323 Buffalo Blankets Cardboard 19½" x 25"

MS-324 Buffalo Pitts Co. Cardboard 24½" x 31"

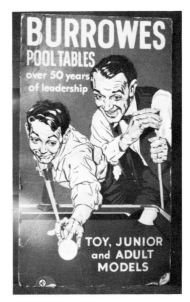

MS-326 Burrows Pool Tables
Cardboard 11" x 18½"

MS-329 B.V.D. Union Suits Tin
13¼" x 9¼"

MS-332 Campbell's Soup Paper

MS-335 Checker Taxi Cardboard 11" x 7"

MS-334 Case Metal
9¼" x 23½"

MS-338 J & P Coats Thread Tin 10" x 14"

MS-343 Comstock's Worm
Pellets Cardboard Stand-up
10" x 13½"

MS-344 Conneaut Can Co.
Tin 14" x 20"

MS-345 Corticelli Spool Silk
Tin Self-Framed 8½" x 10½"

MS-346 E.T. Cowdrey & Co. Tin 14" x 20"

MS-347 E.T. Cowdrey & Co. Tin 14" x 20"

MS-350 Crossman Bros. Seeds
Paper 16" x 23"

MS-352 Cunard Steamers, Garmania Caronia Tin
38½" x 27½"

MS-358 Dependable Hardware Embossed Tin
23½" x 12"

MS-359 DeSoto Six Porcelain Two Sided 48" x 20"

MS-360 Diamond Black
Leather Oil Embossed Tin
20" x 31"

MS-362 Dodge Brothers Porcelain 40" x 17¾"

MS-365 Drugs-Sodas Metal-Slag Glass Inserts Two
Sided Light Up 42" x 21"

MS-367 E-Cut Lingerie Cardboard Stand-up 9¼" x 12½"

MS-375 Enterprise Meat Chopper Paper 14" x 16"

MS-370 El-Bart Gin Tin (with actual chain) 9¼" x 13¼"

MS-373 E.L. St. Aubyn Metal Sign

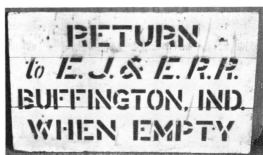

MS-376 Erie Railroad Wood 27" x 15"

MS-378 The Express Porcelain Corner Sign 12" x 15"

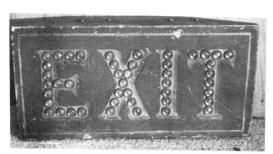

MS-377 Exit Tin Light-up Glass Jeweled Inserts 21" x 10" x 5"

MS-380 N.K. Fairbank & Co.
Paper 15" x 31"

MS-381 Fairbank's Gold Dust Cardboard Stand-up 14½" x 13"

MS-382 Fairy Soap Cardboard 21" x 11"

MS-384 Fairy Soap Cardboard 21" x 11"

MS-385 Fall Tune-up Cardboard 38" x 25"

MS-386 Ferry Seeds Paper
19½" x 28"

MS-387 Ferry's Seeds Paper
19¾" x 27½"

MS-388 Fireman's Insurance Co. Tin 20¼" x 24¼"

MS-389 Firestone Tires Porcelain
Side Mount 21" x 16"

MS-390 Fleischmann's
Yeast Cardboard
12" x 17½"

MS-393 Fontana & Co. Embossed Tin 12" x 16"

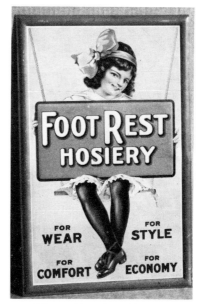

MS-394 Foot Rest Hosiery Tin
11¼" x 17¼"

MS-397 Gem Mops Metal
Die Cut 15" x 23¼"

MS-401 Gold Dust Tin

MS-402 Golden Rod Cereals Tin 35½" x 23"

MS-403 Gold Medal Camp Furniture Tin 18½" x 13½"

MS-404 Goodyear Tires Embossed
Tin 23½" x 11½"

MS-406 Grape Nuts Tin 30½" x 20¼"

MS-407 Grand Union
Tea Co. 1906 Calen-
dar 28½" x 11"

MS-408 Grand
Union Tea Co.
1907 Calendar
29½" x 10"

MS-409 Grand
Union Tea Co.
1905 Calendar
29" x 9½"

MS-410 Griffith & Boyd Co. Aluminium
23½" x 15½"

MS-411 Hall Block Paper 31½" x 23½"

MS-412 Hammar Bros.
White Lead Paper
17" x 13"

MS-413 Hanna's
Enamel Metal
Stand-up
6¼" x 19"

NS-418 Henley Bicycle Paper
13½" x 21¼"

MS-424 Hoadley's Chew-
ing Gum Multi-Layered Tin
Bank 5½" x 11"

MS-428 Hood Rubbers Paper 16" x 23½"

MS-431 Huber Manufactur-
ing Co. Paper 16" x 36"

MS-432 Huntley & Palmers Paper

MS-434 Iron Mountain Route Paper Date 1899 20" x 27"

MS-433 International
Stock Food Paper
9½" x 13½"

MS-435 Ivorine Paper 12" x 16"

MS-436 Ivory Soap Cardboard
14¾" x 19½"

MS-437 Jergen's Soap
Cardboard Hanger
11¼" x 11¼"

MS-441 Johnston
Harvester Co.
1913 Calendar

MS-439 B.J. Johnson & Co. Soaps Tin
16" x 22"

MS-440 Iver Johnson Bicycles Heavy
Cardboard 21" x 11"

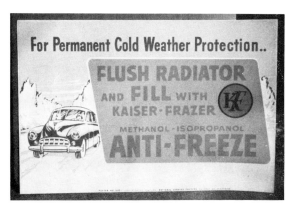

MS-442 Kaiser-Frazer Anti-Freeze Cardboard
38" x 25"

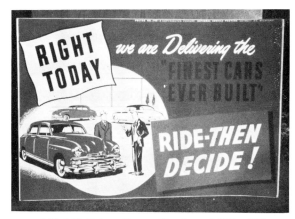

MS-443 Kaiser-Frazer Cardboard 38" x 25"

MS-444 Kaiser-Frazer Luster-Seal Cardboard
38" x 25"

MS-445 Kaiser-Frazer Appearance Treatment
Cardboard 38" x 25"

MS-446 Keds Shoe
Cardboard Stand-up
9" x 16"

MS-447 Keds Shoe Cardboard
Stand-up 12½" x 19½"

MS-449 Kew-Bee Bread Cardboard
Stand-up

MS-452 Kingan's Cardboard 15" x 21"

MS-453 Klages Coal & Ice Co. Metal (Most
were made in cardboard) 8½" x 8½"

MS-456 Kraeuter Tools Metal Die Cut 36" x 10"

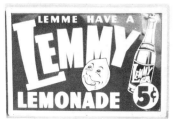

MS-463 Lemmy Lemonade
Embossed Tin 22" x 14½"

MS-457 K.R.O. Cardboard
Stand-up 19¼" x 32"

MS-458 K.R.O. Cardboard
Stand-up 18¾" x 32¾"

MS-459 K-W Season's Greetings Cardboard
38" x 25"

MS-460 K-W Accessories Cardboard 38" x 25"

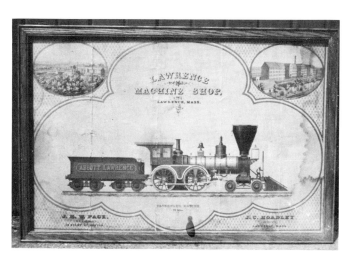

MS-461 Lawrence Machine Shop Heavy Paper 32" x 21"

MS-462 Leggett's Premier Foods Metal
Side Mount 17½" x 13½"

MS-465 Liggett's Chocolates
Cardboard 25" x 31"

MS-467 Lion Coffee Paper
19¾" x 27½"

MS-469 Listman Mill Co. Metal-has been
cut down 21½" x 18½"

MS-470 Livingston & Toney's
Pool Parlor Paper 14" x 19"

MS-473 Lubricate Cardboard 38" x 25"

MS-475 Luxury Coffee
Paper 15¾" x 23"

MS-472 Louney's Cocoa String Holder
Tin 16" x 24"

MS-477 Magee Furnaces-Ranges Cardboard
12" x 14"

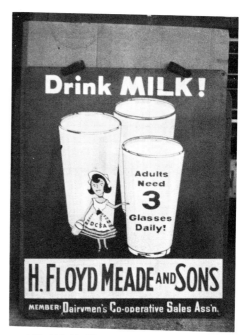

MS-483 H. Floyd Meade & Sons Porcelain 36" x 30"

MS-480 Master Locks
Wood & Metal Board
11½" x 23¼"

MS-484 Meadow Gold Buttermilk Celluloid
13" x 9"

MS-485 Merita Bread Embossed Tin
23" x 34½"

MS-486 Mittag & Volger Embossed Tin

MS-487 Mobilgas Tin
15¾" x 11½"

MS-490 Munsing Wear Metal Die Cut
20½" x 19"

MS-492 Murphy D-Cote Enamel
Tin 18½" x 26¾"

MS-493 Murphy Da-Cote Varnish Tin
18½" x 26¾"

MS-494 Chas. Nober Lumber Co. Paper

MS-495 Natural Set Up Embossed Tin
19½" x 13½"

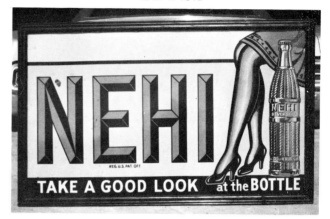

MS-497 Nehi Beverages Tin 59" x 36"

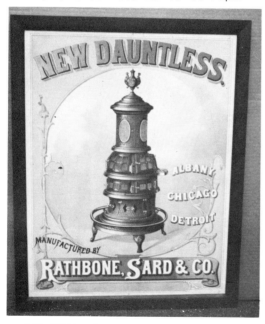

MS-499 New Dauntless Paper 24" x 19¼"

MS-498 Nehi Beverages Tin 56" x 32"

MS-501 New York Underwriters Insurance Co.
Wood - Celluloid Center 26" x 15"

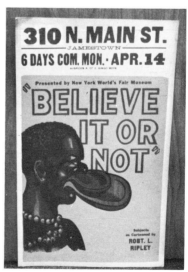

MS-502 New York Worlds
Fair Museum Cardboard
14" x 22"

MS-503 New York World's Fair
Museum Cardboard 14" x 22"

MS-504 Nichol Kola Embossed Tin 18½" x 11"

MS-507 Occident Flour Tin 35½" x 11¾"

MS-506 Annie Oakley Paper

MS-508 Ocean House Inn Metal Side Mount
25½" x 19¼"

MS-509 Old Dutch Cleanser Cardboard
21" x 11"

MS-510 Old Reliable Coffee
Cardboard 21" x 11"

MS-511 Old Reliable Coffee
Cardboard 21" x 11"

MS-512 Old Reliable Coffee Embossed Tin 14" x 6½"

MS-513 Old Reliable Coffee Tin 13" x 6"

MS-514 Old Reliable Coffee
Heavy Paper 33½" x 15½"

MS-515 Old Re-
lialbe Coffee
Cardboard
9¾" x 14¾"

MS-520 Orange
Squeeze Heavy
Cardboard
20½" x 30"

MS-528 Pepsi
Cola Tin 16" x 49"

MS-529 Pepsi
Cola Tin 8" x 29½"

MS-530 Pepsi
Cola Tin 8" x 29½"

MS-523 Packard Wood 25" x 17½"

MS-525 Pennzoil Gasoline Porcelain
30"

MS-532 Pepsi Cola Tin Menu Board
19½" x 30"

MS-531
Pepsi Cola
Embossed
Tin

MS-536 Pirate Plows Paper Date 1890 20½" x 26½"

MS-537 Postal Telegraph Wood 29½" x 26¼"

MS-538 Postal Telegraph Porcelain 30" x 24"

MS-539 Pratts Poultry Regulator Paper
Date 1907 24¼" x 17½"

MS-541 Providence Line Cardboard 12" x 15"

MS-543 Quaker Oats Cardboard 21" x 11"

MS-545 Raybelle Lin-
gerie Cardboard Stand-
up 11¼" x 16¼"

MS-546 Raybestos Metal Side Mount 26" x 20"

MS-547 R.C.A. Radiotrons Tin
23½" x 35"

MS-550 R & G Corsets Tin 16" x 11½"

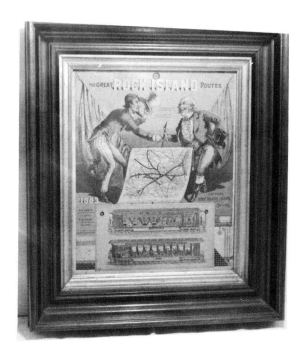

MS-552 Rock Island Railway Cardboard 10" x 14"

MS-551 Rice's Flower Seeds Paper

MS-553 Round Oak Double Burner Paper

MS-556 Sanfords Ink Tin 13½" x 9½"

MS-561 Sealed Power Porcelain 36" x 19"

MS-563 Selz Shoes Wood

MS-565 Selz Shoes Reverse on Glass (Double Glass)
22" x 26"

MS-567 Sheboygan Coffee
Co. Paper 12" x 16"

MS-568 Simonize Cardboard
Stand up 18" x 26"

MS-572 Smith American Organ Paper 24" x 32"

MS-569 Sleepy Eye Flour Tin

MS-570 Sleepy Eye Flour Tin
over Cardboard 13¼" x 19"

MS-576 Spring-Step Cardboard 21" x 11"

MS-573 Sniders Catsup
Tin

194

MS-584 Stewart's Coffee Celluloid 12" x 7"

MS-588 James E. Strates
Shows Cardboard 14" x 22"

MS-589 Sweetest Maid Chocolates Tin Self-Framed
17" x 11½"

MS-590 Swift's Beef Reverse on Glass
34½" x 21"

MS-591 Swift's Borax Paper 13" x 15½"

MS-594 Teutonia Insurance Co. Paper Date
1872 19" x 24"

MS-595 Thomas Inks Tin 13½" x 20"

MS-596 Thurston Hall Co. Paper 23½" x 18½"

MS-601 U.S. Deck Paint
"Pepper Martin" St. Louis
Paper 13¾" x 16¾"

MS-599 Tuft's Arctic Soda Water Paper 14" x 20"

MS-603 Van Houten's Cocoa
Cardboard 31" x 45½"

MS-604 Van Raalte Veils Canvass
12½" x 14½"

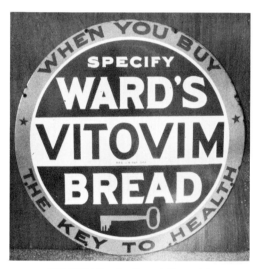

MS-608 Ward's Bread Porcelain
27½"

MS-614 Wells Fargo & Co. Cardboard

MS-613 Welle-Boettler Bakery Porcelain 15" x 36"

MS-615 Wells, Fargo & Co. Reverse on Glass 44" x 33"

MS-619 White Rock Lithia Water
Tin 16¼" x 19½"

MS-620 Williams Extract Cardboard Date 1872 14" x 10¾"

MS-623 D.L. Wing & Co. Paper
13¾" x 19¾"

MS-625 Wood
Key Trade Sign
38" x 13"

MS-624 Wiss Schissors Metal Die Cut 36" x 12"

MS-627 Woonsocket Rubbers Paper 21½" x 32"

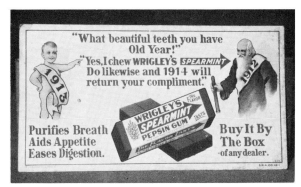

MS-630 Wrigley's Gum Cardboard 21" x 11"

MS-635 Zerolene Oils & Greases Porcelain Side
Mount 24" x 20"

MS-628 World's Fair Freaks
Cardboard 14" x 22"

MS-633 Yeast Foam Card-
board 13¼" x 7½"

MS-634 Youells Rat-Snap Cloth 47" x 35"

TRAYS

TR-214 Akron Brewing Co.
16¾" x 13¾"

TR-218A Bellmore Whiskey 12"

TR-228 Cleveland Buffalo Change
Tray 4¼"

TR-230 Clysmic Water 16 x 13"

TR-241 Abe Freeman Liquor Dealer 16¼ x 12½"

TR-247 R.M. Hunt & Co. Change
Tray 4¼"

TR-250 Leisey Brewing Co. 15" x 2½"

TR-252 Lindquist's Crackers Change Tray
3½" x 5"

TR-252A Lindquist's Crackers Change
Tray 3½" x 5"

TR-253 Moxie Change Tray

TR-256 E. Robinson's Sons Pilsener Beer
12"

TR-267 Thomas' Hay Machinery
Change Tray 4"

TR-269 William Tell Flour Change Tray
4¼"

TOBACCO CUTTERS & LIGHTERS

TCU-32 John Anderson & Co. Cigar
Cutter & Lighter
Iron 6" x 6" x 23"

TCU-33 Artie Cigars
Cutter Iron
6" x 7" x 11"

TCU-34 Banjo Player Iron Cigar
Lighter 5" x 9"

TCU-36 Bloomer Club
Cutter & Lighter Iron
6" x 9" x 18"

TCU-36A Bloomer
Club Cutter & Lighter
Iron 6" x 12" x 12"

TCU-37 Bond Value Cigar Cutter
Iron 7" x 8" x 2½"

TCU-38 Geo. W. Childs Cigar Lighter
Iron 9" x 4" x 10"

TCU-39 Cigar Cutter
& Lighter (Remember
the Maine) Iron
10" x 6" x 14"

TCU-42 Cigar Figure Zinc
14" x 12" x 37"

TCU-41 Cigar Cutter Match Vendor Iron 9½" x 9½"

TCU-43 Cinco Cigar
Lighter Iron 7" x 5" x 12"

TCU-45 Charles
Denby Cigar Lighter
Iron 5" x 4" x 11"

TCU-46 Dexter   TCU-46A Flotilla   TCU-46B Nerve
Cigar Cutters & Lighters Iron 4" x 8" x 10"

TCU-47 Dice Popper Coin
Operated Cigar Cutter Iron

TCU-48 Doremus Cigar Vendor Cutter &
Match Holder 7" x 9" x 15"

TCU-49 Dorsey Cigar
Cutter Iron 8" x 9" x 13½"

TCU-50 Gambling Cigar Cutter Iron
11" x 20" x 8"

TCU-51 El Gemelo Cigar
Cutter & Lighter Iron
10" x 8" x 15"

TCU-52 & 52B Brass Lighters 10"
TCU-52A Gold Seal Matches Iron 3" x 4" x 5"

TCU-53 Gumper Bros. Cigar Cutter
& Trade Stim. Embossed Tin-Die Cut
10" x 15"

TCU-55 Match Dispenser
& Cigar Cutter Iron
6" x 8" x 16"

TCU-56 Match Vendor
Iron

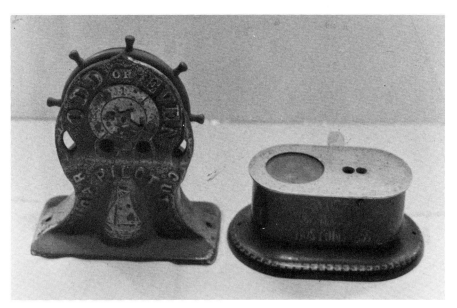

TCU-57 Pilot Cigar Cutter
(Odd or Even) Gambling
Iron 6" x 3" x 7"

TCU-57A Dice Cigar Cutter
Gambling Iron 7" x 4" x 3"

TCU-58 Poet Cigars Cutter
& Lighter Iron 5" x 12" x 14"

TCU-59 Punch Gas Cigar
Lighter Iron 5" x 8"

TCU-60 Reciprocity Cigar
Cutter & Lighter Iron
7" x 10" x 14"

TCU-61 Red Lion
Cigar Cutter Iron
6" x 8" x 4"

TCU-62 Betsy Ross
Cigar Lighter Iron
7" x 12"

TCU-63 Lillian
Russel Cigar Lighter
Iron 7" x 7" x 12"

TCU-64 San Felice
Cigar Lighter Iron
7" x 5" x 12"

TCU-65 Barnes Smith Co. Cigar
Cutter & Lighter Iron 7" x 9" x 20"

TCU-66 Barnes Smith &
Co. Cigar Cutter & Lighter
Iron 6" x 9" x 18"

TCU-67 Sunny Clime
Cigars Cutter & Lighter Iron
9¼" x 18"

TCU-68 Tacoma Cigar Cutter & Lighter Iron
12" x 17"

TCU-71 Uncle Sam
Cigar & Lighter Iron
4½" x 19"

TCU-72 Y-B Cigars Cigar
Lighter 5" x 8" x 8"

TCU-70 Tri-Mount Cigars   TCU-70A Tansill's Punch
TCU-70B C.C.A. Cigars Iron 5" x 9" x 9"

MATCH HOLDERS & STRIKERS

MH-42 Allyn & Blanchard Co.
Tin 4" x 7"

MH-43 Adriance Farm Machinery tin 3½" x 5"

MH-44 American Steel Farm Feuce Tin 3½" x 5"

MH-45 Bengal Furnaces Tin 3½" x 5"

MH-46 Born Steel Range Tin 3½" x 5"

MH-47 Bull Dog Cut Plug Tin 3½" x 6½"

MH-48 Ceresota Flour Tin 3½" x 5"

MH-49 Ceresota Flour Tin 2¼" x 5½"

MH-50 J.L. Clark Mfg. Co. Tin Match Striker 3½" x 5"

MH-51 Columbia
Mill Co. Tin
2¼" x 5½"

MH-52 Dewey Portland
Cement Tin 3½" x 5"

MH-53 Eagle Lye Tin 3½" x 5"

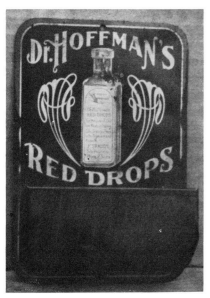

MH-54 Dr. Hoffman's Red Drops Tin
3½" x 5"

MH-55 Holsum Bread Tin
3½" x 5"

MH-56 A. Hussey & Co.
Tin 3½" x 7"

MH-57 Ideal Leather Polish
Tin 4¼" x 5½"

MH-58 Indianapolis Morning Star
Tin 3½" x 5"

MH-59 Key Brand
Shoes Tin 3½" x 5"

MH-60 Laib Co. Supplies
Tin 3½" x 5"

MH-61 Laurel Stoves &
Ranges Tin 3½" x 5"

MH-62 Merry War Lye
Tin 3¾" x 5½"

MH-63 Wm. Miller Range &
Furnace Tin 3½" x 5" x 2¼"

MH-64 Milwaukee Harvesting
Machines Tin 3¼" x 5½"

MH-65 Old Judson Whiskey
Tin 3½" x 5"

MH-66 Othello Range Tin
3½" x 5"

MH-67 Reliance Baking
Powder Tin 4¼" x 5½"

MH-68 Rex Roofing Tin 3½" x 5½"

MH-69 Osborne Line Tin
3½" x 5"

MH-70 W. Spear (Farm Imp-
pement) Wood 5" x 7"

MH-71 Dr. Shoop's
Coffee Tin 3½" x 5"

MH-72 Sunny Brook Rye Tin
3½" x 5"

MH-73 Sunny Brook Rye Tin
3½" x 5"

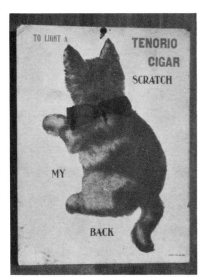

MH-74 Tenorio Cigar Card-
board Match Striker 6½" x 8½"

MH-75 Tenorio Cigar Cardboard
6½" x 8½"

MH-76 Universal Stoves &
Range Tin 3½" x 5"

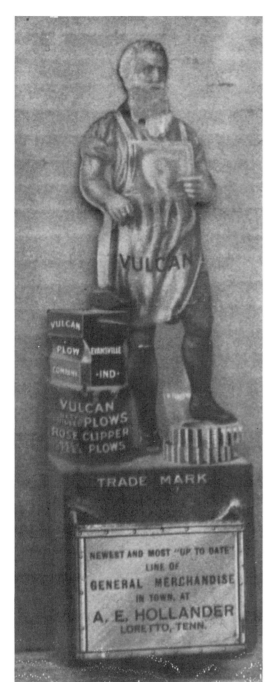

MH-77 Vulcan Plows Tin
2¾" x 7¾"

MH-78 White House Coffee Tin 3½" x 5"

MISCELLANEOUS ITEMS

M-208 Barn Yard Wood & Metal
Case-Play Poker

M-209 Berry Brothers Varnishes
Wood Wagon 27" x 14" x 19"

M-210 Bigelow Weavers Paper Mache

M-211 Bull Dog Garters Paper Mache

M-212 Bull-Meat Flour
Heavy Cardboard 20" x 12"

M-214 Buttermilk Porcelain

M-215 Dr. W. B.
Caldwell's Card-
board Display Box
8" x 20" x 5"

M-216 Carborundum (Sharpening Stones)
Wood Box with Drawers 14½" x 14½" x 7"

M-218 Cherryallen
Metal-Glass
Dispenser

M-219 Collar Button Dispenser
Iron 9" x 9" x 14"

M-221 Dutch Boy Paint Metal
String Holder

M-224 Golden
Sun Coffee Metal
Scoop 4" x 1¾"

M-225 Hires Root
Beer Syrup Disp.
Turn Spout
7¾" x 12"

M-227 Lehman Bros. Chalk
14" x 7" x 17"

M-226 Honest Scrap Cardboard
Packing Box

M-229 Mail Pouch Tobacco
Metal String Holder
15" x 31"

M-236 Sauer's Extracts Embossed Tin Cabinet 12" x 8" x 26"

M-230 Modax Heavy Embossed Glass 5"

M-232 Parker Fountain Pens
Glass Globe Light-up

M-237 Schlitz Brewery
Metal Shade Glass inserts

M-238 Soda Dispenser Metal-Glass

M-241 Terrocotta Cigar Figure
11" x 9" x 26"

M-242 Dr. West's Tooth-
brush Glass Counter Dis-
play Case

M-243 Wood Figure 17" x 26" x 16"

M-244 Zanzibar Nutmeg Wood-
Paper Label 11" x 9½"

DOOR PUSHES

DP-16 American
Special Flour Tin
3½" x 6½"

DP-17 Bakers
Vanilla Tin

DP-18 Burton Brewing
Co. Reverse on Glass
4" x 10"

DP-19 Coca-
Cola Metal
3" x 12"

DP-20 Congress
Beer Porcelain
4" x 6½"

DP-21 Domino Cigaret-
tes Tin 4" x 14"

DP-22 Duke's Mix-
ture Porcelain
4¼" x 8¼"

DP-23 Eveready Tin
3½" x 9"

DP-24 Fast
Mail Overalls
Porcelain
3" x 8"

DP-25 Fleisch-
mann's Yeast Tin
3¼" x 8¾"

DP-26 Frostie Tin
3½" x 6½"

DP-27 J. H. P. Cigar
Porcelain (has match
striker) 4" x 6"

DP-28 Kirk's Flake
Soap Porcelain
4" x 8½"

DP-29 Lawrence
Paints Porcelain
4" x 8"

DP-30 Lighthouse
Cleanser Porcelain
4½" x 7½"

DP-31 Lipton's
Tea Porcelain
3" x 7"

DP-32 Lyon's
Tea Porcelain
3" x 10"

DP-33 Musselman
& Co. Tin 3" x 9½"

DP-34 Necco
Sweets Porcelain
3¾ x 11¼"

DP-35 Orange
Crush Tin
3" x 12"

DP-36 Pay Car
Porcelain 3" x 6"

DP-37 Plow Boy Tobacco
Porcelain 4" x 6½"

DP-38 Recruit Cigars
Porcelain 4" x 8½"

DP-39 Red Man
Porcelain 3" x 6"

DP-40 Red Rose
Tea Porcelain
3" x 9"

DP-41 Salada
Tea Porcelain
2½" x 9¾"

DP-42 Star Naphtha
Porcelain 3½" x 6¼"

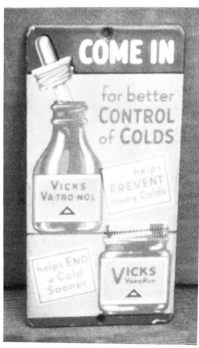

DP-43 Vick's Por-
celain 3¾" x 7½"

DP-44 Wise Potato
Chips Tin 3½" x 6½"

MISC. TIN CONTAINERS

MTC-1 Andy Gump Tin Bank

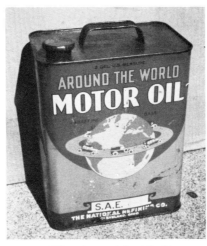

MTC-2 Around the World
Motor Oil 8½" x 5¾" x 10½"

MTC-3 B.Z.B. Oil
9½" x 9½" x 14"

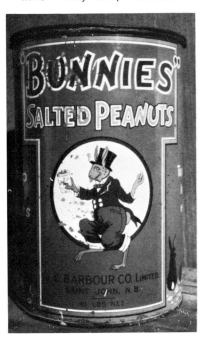

MTC-4 Bunnies Salted Peanuts
10 lbs. 8" x 11"

MTC-5 Bunny Coffee 4 lbs. 7½" x 8"

MTC-6 Continental Oil
8½" x 9½" x 14"

MTC-7 Coreco Motor Oil Metal
14¼" x 8½" x 16½"

MTC-8 Cow-Ease
5" x 5" x 9½"

MTC-9 Dustdown
8½" x 5¼"

MTC-10 En-Ar-Co. Motor Oil
Tin Bank 3" x 3" x 4¼"

MTC-11 Fountain Tobacco
5" x 6¼"

MTC-12 Hitts
Danger Lights
Tin 2¼" x 13"

MTC-13 Jackie
Pencil Box
2" x 7¾" x ¾"

MTC-15 Maryland Beauty
Oysters 7¼" x 6¾"

MTC-16 "Our Own" Cough Drops Store
Bin 9¼" x 12" x 9¼"

MTC-17 Pickaninny Salted Peanuts 10 lbs. 8½" x 9."

MTC-18 Prosit Tobacco Cardboard
8" x 2¼"

MTC-19 Powow Salted Peanuts
8½" x 9¾"

MTC-20 Roger Bean Cigar 5½" x 6" x 4"

MTC-21 Scholl's Axle Grease
6½" x 6"

MTC-22 Shoe Lace Service Station Tin
11¼" x 11¼" x 11"

MTC-23 Smith Bros.
Cough Drops Tin
4¼" x 4¼" x 9¾"

MTC-25 Thresher Hard Oil
9¼" x 9¼" x 9¾"

MTC-24 Switch Cigars
5¼" x 5½"

MTC-26 Uncle Wiggily 3¾" x 3½"

MTC-27 Worden Grocer Co. Store Bin
19" x 13" x 18¾"

GUM, PEANUT, ETC. VENDORS

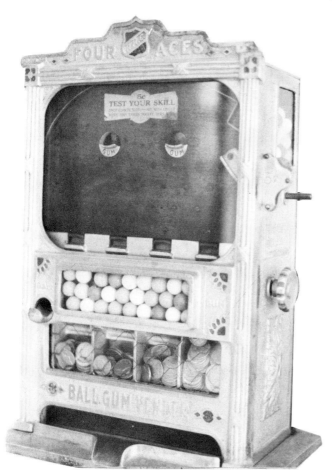

GP-5 Four Aces Ball Gum Vendor Metal
12" x 8" x 16"

GP-4 Daval Trade Stimulator
Metal Case

GP-7 Mills Good Luck Oak
Case

GP-8 Mills Novelty Co. Wood & Iron 9" x 10" x 12"

GP-9 Mills Owl Peanut Vendor
Wood & Iron

GP-10 National Cash
Register

GP-12 Peanut Vendor Iron
10" x 10" x 22"

GP-11 National Lead Pencil Vendor 11½" x 17"

GP-14 Perfume Vendor Wood Date 1897
14" x 5" x 15"

GP-15 Proto Type Gum Vendor
Bronze 10" x 10" x 21"

GP-18 St. Nicholas Pepsin Gum
Wood & Porcelain 10" x 10" x 30"

POT AND PAN SCRAPERS
Sizes Range From:
2¼" x 3¼" — 3¼" x 2½"

PS-13 Junket Desserts

PS-15 King Midas Flour

PS-14 King Midas Flour

PS-16 Mt. Penn Stove Works

PS-17 Nesco

PS-18 Red Wing Milling Co.

PS-19 Royal King Stove

PS-20 Roth's Dove Brand

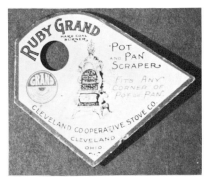

PS-21 Ruby Grand

PS-22 Sharples Cream
Sep.

PS-23 Sharples Cream
Sep.

PS-24 Sunshine Finishes

POT AND PAN SCRAPERS
Sizes Range From:
2¼" x 3¼" — 3¼" x 2½"

PS-1 Admiral Coffee

PS-2 American Maid Bread

PS-3 Babbitt's Cleanser

PS-4 Better Butter

PS-5 Delco-Light

PS-6 Fairmount Creamery

PS-7 Grand Combination Range

PS-8 Grand Gas Range

PS-9 Henkel's Flour

PS-10 Junket Desserts

PS-11 Junket Desserts

PS-12 Junket Desserts

CHRISTMAS PAILS AND TINS

CP-1 Brinckerhoff's 6" x 4" x 2"

CP-2 Compliments of the Season
3¼" x 3¼"

CP-3 Merry Christmas 1898-1899
3¼" x 3¼"

CP-4 Merry Christmas (Ceto
Findner) 3¼" x 3¼"

CP-5 Merry Christmas Happy
New Year 3¼" x 3¼"

CP-6 Merry Christmas-Happy
New Year 2½" x 3"

CP-7 Merry Christmas
Heekin Can Co. 3¼" x 3¼"

CP-8 Merry Christmas
(Hickory Street Church)
3¼" x 3¼"

CP-9 Merry Christmas
(Frank Fischer) 3¼" x 3¼"

CP-10 Merry Christmas (C.E.
Gunther) 3¼" x 3¼"

CP-11 Merry Christmas (C.G.
Hogue) 3¼" x 3¼"

CP-12 Compliments of the
Season (C.G. Hogue)
3¼" x 3¼"

CP-13 Merry Christmas
(Little Chicago) 3¼" x 3¼"

CP-14 Merry Christmas
(Londen Bros.) 3¼" x 3¼"

CP-15 Merry Christmas From Santa
4½" x 2½" x 2¼"

CP-16 Merry Christmas (Jacob
H. Stephens) 3¼" x 3¼"

CP-17 Night Before Christmas 4½" x 2½" x 2¼"

CP-18 Santa 4" x 1¾"

PEANUT BUTTER PAILS

PB-96 Bayle Peanut Butter
3½" x 3½"

PB-97 Beaver Peanut Butter
3¼" x 3½"

PB-98 Betsy Ross Peanut
Butter 3½" x 3¾"

PB-99 Beurre Champlian
Peanut Butter 3½" x 3"

PB-100 Big Sister Peanut Butter
3¾" x 3½"

PB-101 Bluhill Peanut Butter
3½" x 3"

PB-102 Gold Bond Peanut Butter
3¾" x 3½"

PB-103 Golden Drip
Peanut Butter 3¼" x 3½"

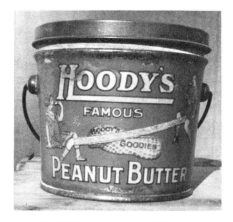

PB-104 Hoddy's Peanut Butter
3¾ x 3½"

PB-105 Jack Sprat Peanut Butter
3½" x 3"

PB-106 Kiddies Peanut Butter
3½" x 3"

PB-107 Meadow Sweet
3½" x 3¾"

PB-108 Minneopa Peanut Butter
4" x 3½"

PB-109 Monarch Peanut Butter
3¼" x 3¾"

PB-110 Morris Supreme
Peanut Butter 3½" x 3¾"

PB-111 Niagara Peanut Butter
3¾" x 3½"

PB-112 Parrot Peanut Butter
3½" x 3½"

PB-113 Scowcraft's Peanut
Butter 4¼" x 4¾"

PB-114 Pedigreed Peanut
Butter 3½" x 3"

PB-115 Planters Peanut
Butter 3½" x 4"

PB-116 School Boy Peanut
Butter 3½" x 3¾"

PB-117 School Days Peanut Butter
3¾" x 3½"

PB-118 Squirrel Peanut Butter
3½" x 3¼"

PB-119 Sunshine Peanut Butter
3½" x 3¾"

PB-120 Sweet Girl Peanut Butter
3½" x 3½"

PB-120A Squirrel Peanut Butter
15 lbs. 8¼" x 8¼"

PB-121 Tropical Peanut Butter
3¾" x 4"

PB-122 Upton's Peanut Butter
3¼" x 3½"

PB-123 White Clover Peanut
Butter 3½" x 3¾"

PB-124 Yacht Club Peanut Butter
3¾" x 3½"

THERMOMETERS

TH-12 A.C.
Spark Plugs
Metal Thermo-
meter

TH-13 Campbell's
Soup Porcelain
7" x 12"

TH-14 Indianapolis Glove Co.
Metal 12"

TH-15 Thermometer
from Building that
Made Kitchen Size
Bronze 8" x 12" x 54"

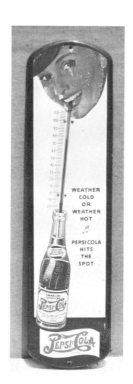

TH-16 Pepsi
Cola Tin

TH-17 Sauer's Wood
3¾" x 8"

CLOCKS

CL-8 General Electric
Refrigerator Clock
Heavy Metal 5¼" x 9"

CL-9 Gibbons Beer Ale Electric
Wall Clock Plastic Case 15½"

CL-10 Liberty Flour Electric
Clock Wood Case Tin Face
15¼" x 15¼"

CL-12 None Such Mince Meat Cardboard & Tin
9½"

CL-11 Mothers Seigel's
Syrup Tin

CL-15 Silver Top Beer Light
Up Clock 15"

ANTIQUE ADVERTISING ENCYCLOPEDIA
Vol. II

The following Price Guide is intended only as a guide. The prices quoted are the top price that a collector will pay for and item needed for his collection.
DEALERS PRICE IS 30% - 50% LESS THAN THE PRICE QUOTED.

BEER & BREWERY SIGNS

BS-135 — $1200	BS-156 — $ 125	BS-178 — $ 550	BS-201 — $1050
BS-136 — $ 850	BS-157 — $ 200	BS-179 — $1000	BS-202 — $ 550
BS-137 — $1800	BS-158 — $1000	BS-180 — $ 195	BS-203 — $1100
BS-138 — $1400	BS-159 — $ 750	BS-181 — $1800	BS-204 — $ 750
BS-139 — $1400	BS-160 — $3000	BS-182 — $ 750	BS-205 — $1000
BS-140 — $1500	BS-161 — $2500	BS-183 — $1600	BS-206 — Rare
BS-141 — $2500	BS-162 — $1800	BS-184 — $ 650	BS-207 — $2000
BS-142 — $3000	BS-163 — Rare	BS-185 — $3500	BS-208 — $ 950
BS-143 — $ 350	BS-164 — $ 400	BS-186 — $ 550	BS-209 — $1200
BS-144 — $ 100	BS-165 — $ 550	BS-187 — $ 950	BS-210 — $1600
BS-145 — $1800	BS-166 — $ 950	BS-188 — $1000	BS-211 — $1200
BS-146 — $ 750	BS-167 — $1600	BS-189 — $ 650	BS-212 — Rare
BS-147 — $ 550	BS-168 — $2800	BS-190 — $ 800	BS-213 — Rare
BS-148 — $ 750	BS-169 — $2450	BS-191 — $ 500	BS-213A— $ 850
BS-149 — $ 650	BS-170 — $ 650	BS-192 — $1000	BS-214 — $ 950
BS-150 — $1000	BS-171 — $ 800	BS-193 — $1600	BS-215 — $ 650
BS-151 — $ 850	BS-172 — $1250	BS-194 — $2800	BS-216 — $ 350
BS-152 — $ 150	BS-172A— $ 750	BS-195 — Rare	BS-217 — $ 175
BS-153 — $ 500	BS-173 — $ 650	BS-196 — $ 650	BS-218 — $ 275
BS-154 — $ 450	BS-174 — $ 550	BS-197 — $ 750	BS-219 — $ 750
BS-155 — $2500	BS-175 — $2500	BS-198 — $1600	BS-220 — $ 850
	BS-176 — $ 650	BS-199 — $ 550	BS-220A— $1400
	BS-177 — $2800	BS-200 — $ 450	BS-221 — $ 450

BS-222 — $ 195
BS-223 — $ 850
BS-224 — $ 850
BS-225 — $1200
BS-226 — $ 500
BS-227 — $ 500
BS-228 — $ 95
BS-229 — $ 450
BS-230 — $1800
BS-231 — $ 500
BS-232 — $ 850
BS-233 — $ 950
BS-234 — $ 750
BS-235 — $ 475
BS-236 — $ 850
BS-237 — $1200
BS-238 — $ 550
BS-239 — $1200
BS-240 — $ 350
BS-241 — $2850
BS-242 — $ 395
BS-243 — $ 650
BS-244 — $ 550
BS-245 — $2000
BS-246 — $ 300

CHRISTMAS PAILS AND TINS
CP- 1 — $ 175
CP- 2 — $ 185
CP- 3 — $ 195
CP- 4 — $ 200
CP- 5 — $ 225
CP- 6 — $ 125
CP- 7 — $ 235
CP- 8 — $ 175
CP- 9 — $ 175
CP-10 — $ 175
CP-11 — $ 185
CP-12 — $ 175
CP-13 — $ 175
CP-14 — $ 200
CP-15 — $ 165
CP-16 — $ 200
CP-17 — $ 125
CP-18 — $ 75

CLOCKS
CL- 1 — $ 950
CL- 2 — $1200
CL- 3 — Rare
CL- 4 — $ 500
CL- 5 — $ 450
CL- 6 — $2500
CL- 7 — $2000
CL- 8 — $ 150
CL- 9 — $ 125
CL-10 — $ 300
CL-11 — $ 195
CL-12 — $ 550
CL-13 — $2200
CL-14 — Rare
CL-15 — $ 150

COCA-COLA ITEMS
CC-34 — $ 300
CC-35 — $ 475
CC-36 — $1200

DOOR PUSHES
DP-16 — $ 125
DP-17 — $ 150
DP-18 — $ 375
DP-19 — $ 250
DP-20 — $ 225
DP-21 — $ 200pr.
DP-22 — $ 225
DP-23 — $ 185
DP-24 — $ 195
DP-25 — $ 195
DP-26 — $ 95
DP-27 — $ 225
DP-28 — $ 195
DP-29 — $ 175
DP-30 — $ 200
DP-31 — $ 195
DP-32 — $ 195
DP-33 — $ 295
DP-34 — $ 225
DP-35 — $ 125
DP-36 — $ 175
DP-37 — $ 375
DP-38 — $ 250
DP-39 — $ 175
DP-40 — $ 185
DP-41 — $ 185
DP-42 — $ 185
DP-43 — $ 195
DP-44 — $ 175

GUM, PEANUT, ETC. VENDORS
GP- 1 — $1000
GP- 2 — $1500
GP- 3 — $1700
GP- 4 — $ 375
GP- 5 — $2800
GP- 6 — Rare
GP- 7 — $ 650
GP- 8 — $ 800
GP- 9 — $3900
GP-10 — $ 850
GP-11 — $2500
GP-12 — $3500
GP-13 — $2000
GP-14 — $1200
GP-15 — $1600
GP-16 — $2500
GP-17 — $5000
GP-18 — Rare
GP-19 — Rare
GP-20 — $1700

GUN POWDER ADVERTISING
GUN- 1 — $1000
GUN- 2 — $1200
GUN- 3 — $1000
GUN- 4 — $ 300
GUN- 5 — $1650
GUN- 6 — $ 800
GUN- 7 — $4500
GUN- 8 — Rare
GUN- 9 — $ 550
GUN-10 — $ 350
GUN-11 — $4000
GUN-12 — $ 350
GUN-13 — $ 750
GUN-14 — $1500
GUN-15 — $1250
GUN-16 — $ 650
GUN-17 — $1000
GUN-18 — $ 900
GUN-19 — $ 195
GUN-20 — $ 850
GUN-21 — $1200
GUN-22 — $ 275
GUN-23 — $1200
GUN-24 — $2500
GUN-25 — $ 350
GUN-26 — $ 850
GUN-27 — $ 395
GUN-28 — $ 395
GUN-29 — $ 395
GUN-30 — $ 650
GUN-31 — $ 650
GUN-32 — $ 650
GUN-33 — $ 250
GUN-34 — $ 550

HEINZ FOOD PRODUCTS CONTAINERS
HF- 1 — $ 300
HF- 2 — $ 350
HF- 3 — $ 400
HF- 4 — $ 325
HF- 5 — $ 500
HF- 6 — $ 300
HF- 7 — $ 350
HF- 8 — $ 375
HF- 9 — $ 500
HF-10 — $ 350
HF-11 — $ 475
HF-12 — $ 325
HF-12A– $ 375
HF-13 — $ 350
HF-14 — $ 475
HF-15 — $ 475
HF-16 — $ 450
HF-17 — $ 350
HF-18 — $ 300
HF-19 — $ 300
HF-20 — $ 475
HF-21 — $ 475
HF-22 — $ 350
HF-23 — $ 350
HF-24 — $ 425
HF-25 — $ 300
HF-26 — $ 375
HF-27 — $ 400
HF-28 — $ 375

MATCH HOLDERS & STRIKERS
MH-42 — $ 300
MH-43 — $ 225
MH-44 — $ 100
MH-45 — $ 175
MH-46 — $ 175
MH-47 — $ 600
MH-48 — $ 275
MH-49 — $ 250
MH-50 — $ 125
MH-51 — $ 650
MH-52 — $ 225
MH-53 — $ 125
MH-54 — $ 200
MH-55 — $ 195
MH-56 — $ 600
MH-57 — $ 195

MH-58 — $ 125
MH-59 — $ 195
MH-60 — $ 195
MH-61 — $ 125
MH-62 — $ 265
MH-63 — $ 225
MH-64 — $ 295
MH-65 — $ 125
MH-66 — $ 150
MH-67 — $ 225
MH-68 — $ 250
MH-69 — $ 125
MH-70 — $ 300
MH-71 — $ 150
MH-72 — $ 125
MH-73 — $ 225
MH-74 — $ 100
MH-75 — $ 100
MH-76 — $ 125
MH-77 — $ 300
MH-78 — $ 175

MEDICINAL SIGNS
MDS- 1 — Rare
MDS- 2 — $ 250
MDS- 3 — $2000
MDS- 4 — $1200
MDS- 5 — $2000
MDS- 6 — $1850
MDS- 7 — $1200
MDS- 8 — $1000
MDS- 9 — $1600
MDS-10 — $1400
MDS-11 — $ 750
MDS-12 — $3500
MDS-13 — $ 850
MDS-14 — $2500
MDS-15 — $1000
MDS-16 — $ 100
MDS-17 — $ 100
MDS-18 — $ 100
MDS-19 — $ 100
MDS-20 — $ 100
MDS-21 — $ 180
MDS-22 — $ 550
MDS-23 — $ 450
MDS-24 — $4500
MDS-24A– $ 295
MDS-25 — $ 125
MDS-26 — $ 195
MDS-27 — $3000
MDS-28 — $3800
MDS-29 — $3500

MDS-30 — $ 300
MDS-31 — $ 800
MDS-32 — $ 850
MDS-33 — $1200
MDS-34 — $ 350
MDS-35 — $ 450
MDS-36 — $1600
MDS-37 — $ 550
MDS-38 — $ 550
MDS-39 — $1500
MDS-40 — $ 550
MDS-41 — $1000
MDS-41A– $ 40
MDS-42 — $ 225
MDS-43 — $ 350
MDS-44 — $ 650
MDS-45 — $ 150
MDS-46 — $ 125
MDS-47 — $ 65
MDS-48 — $ 65
MDS-49 — $ 950
MDS-50 — $ 750
MDS-51 — $ 650
MDS-52 — $3000
MDS-53 — $ 450
MDS-54 — $5500
MDS-55 — $ 550
MDS-56 — $ 850
MDS-57 — $ 950
MDS-58 — $ 750
MDS-59 — $ 850
MDS-60 — $ 750
MDS-61 — $ 250
MDS-62 — $ 850

MISCELLANEOUS ITEMS
M-205 — $ 650
M-206 — Pot $400
    Mugs 35 ea.
M-207 — $ 500
M-213 — $ 750
M-217 — $ 100
M-220 — $2200
M-222 — $1000
M-223 — $2500
M-228 — $ 550
M-231 — $ 500
M-233 — $ 850
M-234 — $3500
M-235 — $1500
M-239 — $2200
M-240 — $ 175

MISCELLANEOUS SIGNS
MS-265 — $ 550
MS-266 — $1200
MS-267 — $1100
MS-268 — $1500
MS-269 — $ 750
MS-270 — $ 275
MS-271 — $ 375
MS-272 — $ 250
MS-273 — $ 595
MS-274 — $ 100
MS-275 — $ 275
MS-276 — $ 550
MS-277 — $3500
MS-278 — $ 250
MS-279 — $ 95
MS-280 — $ 190
MS-281 — $ 650
MS-282 — $1100
MS-283 — $2500
MS-284 — $ 850
MS-285 — $3500
MS-286 — $ 675
MS-287 — $ 650
MS-288 — $ 95
MS-289 — $ 850
MS-290 — $ 700
MS-291 — $ 695
MS-292 — $ 750
MS-293 — $1550
MS-294 — $1000
MS-295 — $ 750
MS-296 — $1800
MS-297 — $ 650
MS-298 — $ 100
MS-299 — $ 850
MS-300 — $ 695
MS-301 — $ 100
MS-302 — $ 295
MS-303 — $ 270
MS-304 — $ 550
MS-305 — $ 850
MS-306 — $ 295
MS-307 — $ 350
MS-308 — $ 125
MS-309 — $ 475
MS-310 — $4500
MS-311 — $ 100
MS-312 — $ 550
MS-313 — $ 650
MS-314 — $ 100
MS-315 — $ 85

MS-316 — $ 950
MS-317 — $ 350
MS-318 — $ 325
MS-319 — $ 350
MS-320 — $1200
MS-321 — $1200
MS-322 — $1100
MS-323 — $ 550
MS-324 — $1000
MS-325 — $ 375
MS-326 — $ 195
MS-327 — $ 450
MS-328 — $2200
MS-329 — $ 300
MS-330 — $2000
MS-331 — $1500
MS-332 — $ 295
MS-333 — $8500
MS-334 — $ 650
MS-335 — $ 175
MS-336 — $ 695
MS-337 — $ 395
MS-338 — $ 650
MS-339 — $ 750
MS-340 — $ 950
MS-341 — $ 450
MS-342 — $ 850
MS-343 — $ 100
MS-344 — $ 350
MS-345 — $ 750
MS-346 — $1200
MS-347 — $1600
MS-348 — $ 450
MS-349 — $ 200
MS-350 — $ 450
MS-351 — $1500
MS-352 — $ 750
MS-353 — $ 550
MS-354 — $ 335
MS-355 — $ 650
MS-356 — $1000
MS-357 — $ 550
MS-358 — $2500
MS-359 — $ 450
MS-360 — $2500
MS-361 — $1000
MS-362 — $ 250
MS-363 — $2800
MS-364 — $ 275
MS-365 — $ 850
MS-366 — $ 375
MS-367 — $ 195
MS-368 — $2500

MS-369 — $ 850	MS-423 — $ 800	MS-475 — $ 250	MS-528 — $ 260
MS-370 — $ 395	MS-424 — $ 750	MS-476 — $ 800	MS-529 — $ 250
MS-371 — $ 350	MS-425 — $ 950	MS-477 — $ 750	MS-530 — $ 175
MS-372 — $ 250	MS-426 — $ 850	MS-478 — $1500	MS-531 — $ 650
MS-373 — $ 750	MS-427 — $ 550	MS-479 — $ 750	MS-532 — $ 150
MS-374 — $ 350	MS-428 — $ 500	MS-480 — $ 480	MS-533 — $ 175
MS-375 — $ 650	MS-429 — $1800	MS-481 — $2500	MS-534 — $2500
MS-376 — $ 125	MS-430 — $ 650	MS-482 — $ 350	MS-535 — $4500
MS-377 — $ 150	MS-431 — $ 850	MS-483 — $ 75	MS-536 — $1500
MS-378 — $ 250	MS-432 — $ 600	MS-484 — $ 85	MS-537 — $1800
MS-379 — $ 850	MS-433 — $ 200	MS-485 — $1500	MS-538 — $ 475
MS-380 — $2500	MS-434 — $1600	MS-486 — $ 650	MS-539 — $ 250
MS-381 — $ 550	MS-435 — $ 350	MS-487 — $ 75	MS-540 — $3350
MS-382 — $ 150	MS-436 — $ 375	MS-488 — $ 750	MS-541 — $ 425
MS-383 — $ 450	MS-437 — $ 150	MS-489 — $ 595	MS-542 — $ 650
MS-384 — $ 250	MS-438 — $ 495	MS-490 — $1600	MS-543 — $ 150
MS-385 — $ 75	MS-439 — $1400	MS-491 — $1500	MS-544 — $1500
MS-386 — $ 450	MS-440 — $ 150	MS-492 — $ 450	MS-545 — $ 100
MS-387 — $ 475	MS-441 — $ 175	MS-493 — $ 150	MS-546 — $ 75
MS-388 — $1500	MS-442 — $ 75	MS-494 — $ 250	MS-547 — $ 250
MS-389 — $ 195	MS-443 — $ 75	MS-495 — $ 175	MS-548 — $ 250
MS-390 — $ 200	MS-444 — $ 75	MS-496 — $ 175	MS-549 — $ 450
MS-391 — $ 850	MS-445 — $ 45	MS-497 — $ 150	MS-550 — $ 275
MS-392 — $ 450	MS-446 — $ 75	MS-498 — $ 150	MS-551 — $ 575
MS-393 — $2500	MS-447 — $ 100	MS-499 — $ 350	MS-552 — $ 450
MS-394 — $ 350	MS-448 — $2200	MS-500 — $ 450	MS-553 — $ 750
MS-396 — $1500	MS-449 — $ 150	MS-501 — $ 195	MS-554 — $ 800
MS-397 — $1200	MS-450 — $ 850	MS-502 — $ 75	MS-555 — $1325
MS-398 — $ 750	MS-451 — $ 550	MS-503 — $ 75	MS-556 — $ 395
MS-399 — $ 850	MS-452 — $ 350	MS-504 — $ 75	MS-557 — $ 450
MS-400 — Rare	MS-453 — $ 45	MS-505 — $3500	MS-558 — $ 650
MS-401 — $3800	MS-454 — $ 195	MS-506 — $1400	MS-559 — $ 750
MS-402 — $ 650	MS-455 — $ 500ea.	MS-507 — $ 75	MS-560 — $1800
MS-403 — $ 600	MS-456 — $1000	MS-508 — $ 100	MS-561 — $ 195
MS-404 — $ 195	MS-457 — $ 225	MS-509 — $ 75	MS-562 — $ 450
MS-405 — $ 495	MS-458 — $ 250	MS-510 — $ 100	MS-563 — $ 225
MS-406 — $2500	MS-459 — $ 75	MS-511 — $ 125	MS-564 — $ 250
MS-407 — $ 250	MS-460 — $ 75	MS-512 — $ 75	MS-565 — $ 750
MS-408 — $ 250	MS-461 — $ 450	MS-513 — $ 85	MS-566 — $1200
MS-409 — $ 250	MS-462 — $ 150	MS-514 — $ 175	MS-567 — $ 275
MS-410 — $ 150	MS-463 — $ 65	MS-515 — $ 75	MS-568 — $ 100
MS-411 — $ 600	MS-464 — $ 395	MS-516 — $ 750	MS-569 — $1800
MS-412 — $ 200	MS-465 — $ 125	MS-517 — $3500	MS-570 — $1000
MS-413 — $ 150	MS-466 — $3000	MS-518 — $ 350	MS-571 — $ 800
MS-414 — $ 65	MS-467 — $ 500	MS-519 — $ 325	MS-572 — $ 590
MS-415 — $ 395	MS-468 — $ 550	MS-520 — $ 195	MS-573 — $ 350
MS-416 — $1500	MS-469 — $ 450	MS-521 — $1250	MS-574 — $ 650
MS-417 — $2400	Full Size 1500	MS-522 — $2200	MS-575 — $1200
MS-418 — $ 550	MS-470 — $ 495	MS-523 — $ 400	MS-576 — $ 100
MS-419 — $ 550	MS-471 — $ 550	MS-524 — $2400	MS-577 — $1200
MS-420 — $ 650	MS-472 — $3000	MS-525 — $ 250	MS-578 — $ 250
MS-421 — $ 450	MS-473 — $ 75	MS-526 — $ 350	MS-579 — $ 550
MS-422 — $ 495	MS-474 — $ 750	MS-527 — $ 550	MS-580 — $ 650

MS-581 — $ 600	**MISC. TIN**	MO-22 — $ 400	MA- 43 — $ 90
MS-582 — $2000	**CONTAINER**	MO-23 — $ 350	MA- 44 — $ 60
MS-583 — $ 350	MTC- 1 — $ 175	MO-24 — $ 100	MA- 45 — $ 60
MS-584 — $ 100	MTC- 2 — $ 75	MO-25 — $ 150	MA- 46 — $ 60
MS-585 — Rare	MTC- 3 — $ 95	MO-26 — $ 450	MA- 47 — $ 65
MS-586 — $1800	MTC- 4 — $ 275	MO-27 — $ 300	MA- 48 — $ 70
MS-587 — $ 650	MTC- 5 — $ 450	MO-28 — $1200	MA- 49 — $ 55
MS-588 — $ 75	MTC- 6 — $ 75	MO-29 — $ 250	MA- 50 — $ 75
MS-589 — $ 750	MTC- 7 — $ 75		MA- 51 — $ 125
MS-590 — $1500	MTC- 8 — $ 150	**MUSIC**	MA- 52 — $ 55
MS-591 — $ 550	MTC- 9 — $ 60	**ADVERTISING**	MA- 53 — $ 60
MS-592 — $ 395	MTC-10 — $ 75	MA- 1 — $ 165	MA- 54 — Rare
MS-593 — $ 550	MTC-11 — $ 450	MA- 2 — $ 70	MA- 55 — $ 350
MS-594 — $1500	MTC-12 — $ 100	MA- 3 — $ 65	MA- 56 — $ 155
MS-595 — $1500	MTC-13 — $ 50	MA- 4 — $ 75	MA- 57 — $ 125
MS-596 — $1200	MTC-14 — $5000	MA- 5 — $ 75	MA- 58 — $ 150
MS-597 — $ 250	MTC-15 — $ 65	MA- 6 — $ 75	MA- 59 — $ 75
MS-598 — $ 450	MTC-16 — $ 375	MA- 7 — $ 165	MA- 60 — $ 100
MS-599 — $ 550	MTC-17 — $ 275	MA- 8 — $ 250	MA- 61 — $ 100
MS-600 — $1200	MTC-18 — $ 195	MA- 9 — $ 175	MA- 62 — $ 95
MS-601 — $ 225	MTC-19 — $ 350	MA- 10 — $ 100	MA- 63 — $ 80
MS-602 — $1500	MTC-19A– Rare	MA- 11 — $ 100	MA- 64 — $ 95
MS-603 — $ 575	MTC-20 — $ 650	MA- 12 — $ 60	MA- 65 — $ 175
MS-604 — $ 250	MTC-21 — $ 75	MA- 13 — $ 75	MA- 66 — $ 125
MS-605 — $1100	MTC-22 — $1200	MA- 14 — $ 65	MA- 67 — $ 145
MS-606 — $ 550	MTC-23 — $ 350	MA- 15 — $ 65	MA- 68 — $ 50
MS-607 — $ 850	MTC-24 — $ 250	MA- 16 — $ 165	MA- 69 — $ 250
MS-608 — $ 165	MTC-25 — $ 135	MA- 17 — $ 150	MA- 70 — $ 85
MS-609 — $3800	MTC-26 — $ 450	MA- 18 — $ 200	MA- 71 — $ 85
MS-610 — $ 550	MTC-27 — $ 750	MA- 19 — $ 40	MA- 72 — $ 85
MS-611 — $ 450		MA- 20 — $ 55	MA- 73 — $ 135
MS-612 — $ 250	**MOXIE ITEMS**	MA- 21 — $ 35	MA- 74 — $ 150
MS-613 — $ 450	MO- 1 — $ 250	MA- 22 — $ 45	MA- 75 — $ 200
MS-614 — $ 350	MO- 2 — $ 295	MA- 23 — $ 60	MA- 76 — $ 225
MS-615 — Rare	MO- 3 — $ 275	MA- 24 — $ 60	MA- 77 — $ 225
MS-616 — $ 550	MO- 4 — $ 275	MA- 25 — $ 75	MA- 78 — $ 75
MS-617 — $ 450	MO- 5 — $ 550	MA- 26 — $ 495	MA- 79 — $ 145
MS-618 — $1800	MO- 6 — $1000	MA- 27 — $ 750	MA- 80 — $ 85
MS-619 — $ 650	MO- 7 — $ 350	MA- 28 — $ 85	MA- 81 — $ 75
MS-620 — $ 275	MO- 8 — $ 800	MA- 29 — $ 55	MA- 82 — $ 250
MS-621 — $ 650	MO- 9 — $ 450	MA- 30 — $ 60	MA- 83 — $ 125
MS-622 — $ 350	MO-10 — $1200	MA- 31 — $ 80	MA- 84 — $ 50
MS-623 — $ 395	MO-11 — $ 295	MA- 32 — $ 110	MA- 85 — $ 120
MS-624 — $1000	MO-12 — Rare	MA- 33 — $ 70	MA- 86 — $ 85
MS-625 — $ 450	MO-13 — $ 350	MA- 34 — $ 60	MA- 87 — $ 125
MS-626 — $ 850	MO-14 — $ 450	MA- 35 — $ 135	MA- 88 — $ 375
MS-627 — $ 550	MO-15 — $ 395	MA- 36 — $ 60	MA- 89 — $ 250
MS-628 — $ 100	MO-16 — $ 350	MA- 37 — $ 85	MA- 90 — $ 475
MS-630 — $ 100	MO-17 — $ 595	MA- 38 — $ 125	MA- 91 — $ 650
MS-631 — $1600	MO-18 — $ 650	MA- 39 — $ 65	MA- 92 — $ 90
MS-633 — $ 195	MO-19 — $ 295	MA- 40 — $ 100	MA- 93 — $ 100
MS-634 — $ 195	MO-20 — $ 250	MA- 41 — $ 75	MA- 94 — $ 95
MS-635 — $ 295	MO-21 — $ 195	MA- 42 — $ 125	MA- 95 — $ 85

MA- 96 — $ 150	PB-101 — $ 125	**THERMOMETERS**	TCU-69 — $ 850
MA- 97 — $ 200	PB-102 — $ 125	TH-12 — $ 175	TCU-70 — $ 300
MA- 98 — $ 75	PB-103 — $ 175	TH-13 — $1200	TCU-70A- $ 300
MA- 99 — $ 175	PB-104 — $ 175	TH-14 — $ 100	TCU-70B- $ 300
MA-100 — $ 75	PB-105 — $ 250	TH-15 — Rare	TCU-71 — $ 450
MA-101 — $ 165	PB-106 — $ 125	TH-16 — $ 275	TCU-72 — $ 650
MA-102 — $ 135	PB-107 — $ 125	TH-17 — $ 150	
MA-103 — $ 95	PB-108 — $ 185		
MA-104 — $ 125	PB-109 — $ 175	**TOBACCO**	**TOBACCO SIGNS**
MA-105 — $ 25	PB-110 — $ 150	**CUTTERS &**	TS-161 — $ 850
MA-106 — $ 400	PB-111 — $ 100	**LIGHTERS**	TS-162 — $ 350
MA-107 — $ 125	PB-112 — $ 300	TCU-32 — $1250	TS-163 — $ 475
MA-108 — $ 125	PB-113 — $ 225	TCU-33 — $ 700	TS-164 — $ 295
MA-109 — $ 125	PB-114 — $ 250	TCU-34 — $ 750	TS-165 — $ 450
MA-110 — $ 125	PB-115 — $ 450	TCU-35 — $ 750	TS-166 — $ 675
MA-111 — $ 85	PB-116 — $ 125	TCU-36 — $ 550	TS-167 — $ 450
MA-112 — $ 200	PB-117 — $ 200	TCU-36A- $ 750	TS-168 — $ 950
MA-113 — $ 75	PB-118 — $ 185	TCU-37 — $ 450	TS-169 — $ 550
MA-114 — $ 60	PB-119 — $ 100	TCU-38 — $1200	TS-170 — $ 450
MA-115 — $ 125	PB-120 — $ 350	TCU-39 — $ 550	TS-171 — $ 850
MA-116 — $ 135	PB-120A- $ 300	TCU-40 — $ 750	TS-172 — $ 650
MA-117 — $ 60	PB-121 — $ 125	TCU-41 — $ 375	TS-173 — $ 395
MA-118 — $ 60	PB-122 — $ 150	TCU-42 — $4500	TS-173A- $8500
MA-119 — $ 60	PB-123 — $ 150	TCU-43 — $ 450	TS-174 — $ 675
MA-120 — $ 75	PB-124 — $ 225	TCU-45 — $ 550	TS-175 — $ 750
MA-121 — $ 75		TCU-46 — $ 450	TS-176 — $2000
MA-122 — $ 60		TCU-46A- $ 450	TS-177 — $ 595
MA-123 — $ 60	**POT AND PAN**	TCU-46B- $ 450	TS-178 — $ 425
MA-124 — $ 60	**SCRAPERS**	TCU-47 — Rare	TS-179 — $ 595
MA-125 — $ 175	PS- 1 — $ 160	TCU-48 — $2500	TS-180 — $ 950
MA-126 — $ 125	PS- 2 — $ 250	TCU-49 — $ 450	TS-181 — $ 475
MA-127 — $ 60	PS- 3 — $ 200	TCU-50 — $3100	TS-182 — $ 450
MA-128 — $ 85	PS- 4 — $ 125	TCU-51 — $ 550	TS-183 — $ 275
MA-129 — $ 70	PS- 5 — $ 125	TCU-52 — $ 150	TS-184 — $ 550
MA-130 — $ 75	PS- 6 — $ 125	TCU-52A- $ 250	TS-185 — $ 550
MA-131 — $ 25	PS- 7 — $ 125	TCU-52B- $ 150	TS-186 — $ 450
MA-132 — $ 250	PS- 8 — $ 125	TCU-53 — $3500	TS-187 — $2500
MA-133 — $ 40	PS- 9 — $ 100	TCU-54 — $ 200	TS-188 — $ 295
MA-134 — $ 175	PS-10 — $ 175	TCU-55 — $1200	TS-189 — $ 375
MA-135 — $ 225	PS-11 — $ 175	TCU-56 — $ 250	TS-190 — $ 750
MA-136 — $ 45	PS-12 — $ 195	TCU-57 — $ 350	TS-191 — $ 550
MA-137 — $ 250	PS-13 — $ 195	TCU-57A- $ 450	TS-192 — $ 200
MA-138 — $ 175	PS-14 — $ 125	TCU-58 — $ 450	TS-193 — $ 275
MA-139 — $ 300	PS-15 — $ 175	TCU-59 — $ 600	TS-194 — $ 850
MA-140 — $ 125	PS-16 — $ 85	TCU-60 — $ 450	TS-195 — $ 450
MA-141 — $ 75	PS-17 — $ 250	TCU-61 — $ 300	TS-196 — $ 275
	PS-18 — $ 150	TCU-62 — $ 375	TS-197 — $ 250
PEANUT BUTTER	PS-19 — $ 125	TCU-63 — $ 350	TS-198 — $2800
PB- 96 — $ 175	PS-20 — $ 200	TCU-64 — $ 350	TS-199 — $3500
PB- 97 — $ 350	PS-21 — $ 125	TCU-65 — $ 750	TS-200 — $ 375
PB- 98 — $ 225	PS-22 — $ 125	TCU-66 — $ 450	TS-201 — $ 575
PB- 99 — $ 125	PS-23 — $ 125	TCU-67 — $ 600	TS-202 — $ 250
PB-100 — $ 225	PS-24 — $ 100	TCU-68 — $ 850	TS-203 — $1500

TS-204 — $ 650	TR-214 — $ 750	TR-241 — $ 700	**WHISKEY SIGNS**
TS-205 — $ 375	TR-215 — $ 500	TR-242 — $ 100	WS- 83 — $ 850
TS-206 — $ 250	TR-216 — $ 295	TR-243 — $ 175	WS- 84 — $ 250
TS-207 — $ 275	TR-217 — $ 225	TR-244 — $ 850	WS- 85 — $2800
TS-208 — $4500	TR-218 — $ 175	TR-245 — $ 250	WS- 86 — $ 850
TS-209 — $ 350	TR-218A — $ 350	TR-246 — $ 250	WS- 87 — $1800
TS-210 — $ 550	TR-219 — $ 675	TR-247 — $ 75	WS- 88 — $ 550
TS-211 — $ 150	TR-220 — $ 850	TR-249 — $ 750	WS- 89 — $ 850
TS-212 — $ 750	TR-221 — $ 295	TR-250 — $ 500	WS- 90 — $ 350
TS-213 — $ 450	TR-222 — $ 450	TR-251 — $ 450	WS- 91 — $1500
TS-214 — $ 595	TR-223 — $ 395	TR-252 — $ 90	WS- 92 — $5500
TS-215 — $1200	TR-224 — $ 450	TR-253 — $ 800	WS- 93 — $ 495
TS-216 — $2000	TR-225 — $ 275	TR-254 — $ 200	WS- 94 — $5500
TS-217 — $2800	TR-226 — $ 550	TR-255 — $ 250	WS- 95 — $ 600
TS-218 — $ 850	TR-227 — Rare	TR-256 — $ 400	WS- 96 — $1800
TS-219 — $ 195	TR-228 — $ 300	TR-257 — $ 350	WS- 97 — $2500
TS-220 — $ 950	TR-229 — $ 550	TR-258 — Rare	WS- 98 — $ 395
TS-221 — $1800	TR-230 — $ 495	TR-259 — $ 125	WS- 99 — $ 850
TS-222 — $4500	TR-231 — $ 350	TR-260 — $ 275	WS-100 — $ 595
TS-223 — $ 250	TR-232 — $ 225	TR-262 — $ 200	WS-101 — $4500
TS-224 — $1800	TR-233 — $ 550	TR-263 — $ 300	WS-102 — $ 550
TS-225 — $ 250	TR-234 — $ 250	TR-264 — $ 250	WS-103 — $ 850
	TR-235 — $ 275	TR-265 — $ 400	WS-104 — $2500
	TR-236 — $ 850	TR-266 — $ 195	WS-105 — $1500
TRAYS	TR-237 — $ 225	TR-267 — $ 100	WS-106 — $ 750
TR-212 — $ 450	TR-238 — $ 400	TR-268 — $ 195	WS-107 — Rare
TR-213 — $ 750	TR-240 — $ 550	TR-269 — $ 100	WS-108 — $3500